Advanced Table Tennis

Advanced Table Tennis

Jack Carr

CORNERSTONE LIBRARY • NEW YORK

CORNERSTONE LIBRARY PUBLICATIONS
Are Distributed By
Simon & Schuster Inc.
630 Fifth Avenue
New York, New York 10020

Manufactured in the United States of America
under the supervision of
Rolls Offset Printing Co., Inc., N. Y.

Preface

Advanced Table Tennis was written to assist in developing a mediocre player into a top-ranking tournament player. It is, therefore, assumed that the reader will already have a good knowledge of the various strokes; since most of these have been adequately described in various books (*see* Bibliography), they are described herein only when other sourccs give insufficient detail. Most of the information in this book is not included in any publication readily available on this continent.

Since table tennis was first organized internationally, the style of play has progressed through three main stages: During the first few years after the International Table Tennis Federation was founded in Germany in 1926, the principal stroke was the half volley or close-table block. This style was largely eclipsed by the chop defender, a style which slowed down the game by allowing the player to stand farther from the table—often fifteen or twenty feet. The third period is still with us. It began in 1952 when the Japanese, armed with sponge rackets and penhold grips, demonstrated that all-out attack was too good for the defenders of that day.

The effect of sponge rubber has now been felt in every continent, and it has caused many changes in strokes and tactics in the western hemisphere. These changes are discussed in this book in detail, since they are not covered to any great extent in any other book commonly found in the United States.

Other chapters not usually found in textbooks discuss mental attitude, health, diet and training. All of these subjects are too broad for an exhaustive coverage, but some of the more important points have been included. A few terms must now be defined before our main subject matter can be introduced. The term *sponge* means either ordinary sandwich rubber or the inverted type; "pimpled rubber" will normally be abbreviated *rubber* wherever this is unambiguous. The sponge racket has brought with it two essentially new strokes—the *loop* and the *lob*. The loop or loop drive is an offensive stroke, usually imparting less speed to the ball than a drive, but with much more topspin that tends to cause the return to be high. It is performed by stroking the ball tangentially and usually more vertically. The loop is very effective against backspin strokes. The lob is a defensive topspin stroke executed in a similar manner to the loop; the stroke is always almost vertical, and the ball arcs 10-15 feet high. The lob is used to return hard drives and kills without presenting the opponent with an opportunity to loop. The *push* or chisel is simply an over-the-table chop of a chop, backspin against backspin. *Hand action* merely means what many books call "wrist" or "wrist motion."

Acknowledgments

In acknowledgment of their assistance in the preparation of this book, I wish to thank the following people:

The United States Table Tennis Association (USTTA) Executive Committee, whose encouragement and solicitation for this book has been inspirational.

Si Wasserman, former USTTA Executive Vice President and Coaching Committee Chairman, whose initial editing led to its final format.

Frank Rohter PhD, Assistant Professor and Director of Exercise Physiology Laboratory, Florida State University, who contributed the chapter, "The Physiology of Performance."

Bill Toomey, U.S. Decathlon Champion and World Record holder, for the contribution of the chapter, "Diet for the Athlete."

Dick Yamaoka, ranking Japanese player and Coaching Committee member, for his chapter, "Racket Surfaces."

Malcolm Anderson, USTTA Photography Committee Chairman, who supplied all of the sequence photographs.

Brooke Williams, high ranking woman player and U.S. World Team member, whose liaison work in obtaining experts to contribute special chapters has made possible a complete text.

Santa Barbara News-Press, for allowing use of the photographs of Miss Williams.

Sue Melton, technical assistant for administration.

Jack Carr

Contents

Advanced Table Tennis

1/Inside Table Tennis

SHAKEHAND OR PENHOLD

It is not the intention of this book to tell you which grip is better, a subject that even world champions will debate. Many of the pros and cons of each grip, however, are accepted by almost everyone. The shakehand grip, for instance, is generally conceded to be more suited to backhand topspin strokes, although the player using the penholder grip can produce a very acceptable backhand drive, especially if his variant of the grip forces the fingertips against the blade. This so-called disadvantage, however, is not what it seems, once one frankly admits that even shakehanders rarely possess truly good backhand drives.

Many claim that all forehand topspin strokes are performed better with the penhold grip. This grip is said to permit more hand action, resulting in increased speed, spin, and deception. There is little doubt, however, that the strokes are as graceful as those of the shakehand grip, if not more so, and they are just as natural.

The penhold grip gives a player no center-position weakness when he changes from the forehand to the backhand, since only one side of the racket is used. This is especially important on shots that are close to the table. The half-volley (block) and push are therefore at least as well, if not better, suited to the penhold grip; last minute finger action in these shots gives a further advantage to the penholder. The penholder may also have an advantage on the service, although it is difficult to tell which grip permits the greater variety.

Contrary to general belief, a perfectly good chop can be made with the penhold grip. Since almost all of the world's best defensive players use the shakehand grip, however, it does appear to be better for a backspin game. Furthermore, even a beginning penholder has a natural tendency to block or drive, whereas the shakehand user will block or push. Almost all the world's top men are attackers.

All but one of the men's singles winners in the world championships since 1952 have been penholders. Together with the above observations, this suggests that the penhold grip is superior. Other considerations, however, cast some doubt on this conclusion. For instance, Brazil has a predominant number of penholders but has produced only one world-class player; and Brazil has never been a power on the international scene. Again, in countries where the penhold grip is used, the sport happens to be more popular and the competition keener than where the shakehand grip predominates; the ranking players there enjoy much more respect and admiration than they do in the United States. All of this serves to attract young, talented players who are willing to work hard and stay with the game. Ultimately, this must result in more world-class players.

In short, it is difficult to recommend one grip over the other. Regardless of which grip is selected, however, the player should have the feel of holding the blade, the handle being used only for additional support. If the penholders appear to have a better ball control, it is because they usually do not hold the handle at all. They hold the blade.

There is no one way to hold the blade in either grip, however. A player should always experiment at first by varying the positions of his thumb, index finger, and the other fingers. The first position that a player adopts will always seem to be the more comfortable when he begins to experiment, but it may not be the best position for his game. Two players seldom have the same grip, just as they seldom stroke the ball in the same way, so experiment is a necessity; it is not enough merely to see how other players do it. The player should also remember that the best grip for one shot may not be the best grip for another; slight changes in the positions of the thumb and index finger between the forehand and the backhand are quite common, although they should be kept to a minimum.

Similarly, the grip can change between attack and defense although here again the change should be kept to a minimum. It is most important to grasp the blade of the racket for an attacking game, but a looser grip, more on the handle, may slow the ball for a better defensive game.

SPONGE OR RUBBER?

Table tennis is a game of spin. Its players are of two fundamental types: those whose games are dependent on applying spin and, often, speed—usually as much as possible—and those whose first objective is a neutralization of the opponent's spin and speed. Almost by definition, these can be reclassified as those players who attack and those who defend.

The player whose game is based on spin will find a distinct advantage in a racket surface that grips the ball. Sponge, with its high resiliency and high coefficient of friction, not only adds more spin than rubber, but also more speed. It is therefore the choice of the topspin attacker. Its advantage is manifested by its easier lift, as in drives; its greater speed, also as in drives; its greater variation, as in the push, chop and service; and its added deception, especially in spin and direction. Add to this the fact that sponge comes in a myriad of types, making it easier to select one for a particular style of play, and it becomes obvious that sponge is superior, at least for an aggressive game.

The defender's first concern, however, is to make sure that his opponent's spin does not unduly trouble him. He needs a racket surface that will grip the ball only enough to give him some control, without so high a co-efficient of friction that the tremendous spin of the attacker will cause the ball to rebound at unwanted angles. His choice is rubber. A few players who rely primarily on the attack style of play also prefer rubber, claiming that it gives them better "feel" and control. They say that it gives them adequate spin and speed variation, and that the extra spin given by sponge causes them to lose control. It may be significant, however, that while almost all the international defenders use rubber, not one top attacker does. The defenders find that their chops have a lower trajectory with rubber, and they can play a more relaxed pushing game; the ball seems to have a tendency to slide on the rubber, so that the spin has less effect. For the same reason, users of rubber feel that an error will not cause as much damage to the placement of the ball.

Because of the different characteristics of the two types of racket surfaces, they necessitate the use of different strokes. For instance, in driving with sponge against chop, the racket should be more closed (i.e., the top should be farther towards the net than the bottom, and the ball should be contacted higher above its mid-point) than with rubber. In addition, the drive stroke and follow-through with sponge will be in a more forward direction than with rubber, and any horizontal part of the swing should be at the end rather than at the beginning. The defensive backspin strokes are also different. The sponge stroke when chopping or pushing is more forward than with rubber, and the follow-through can be horizontal or even slightly upwards.

Since sponge imparts spin more readily, greater practice is needed for the player to learn to control this increased spin. On the other hand, the added resiliency of sponge enables him to return almost any ball that can be reached, without the full stroke that rubber would demand. This resiliency can be utilized to convert a passive half volley into a more aggressive shot, if the player adds a slight upward and forward pushing motion.

Because of the extra speed imparted by sponge, it forces defenders farther back and therefore permits a more effective drop shot. Furthermore, the extra spin tends to make the defender's returns higher, thus making further attack easier. The attacker must bear in mind, however, that his increased topspin comes back as an increased backspin on the chop, so that vigorous attack of more than a few balls in succession can be risky.

Whichever type of surface is selected, the choice of racket itself should be made very carefully. A player should select his racket on the basis of his game and the "feel," i.e., weight, balance and handle shape of the rackets available; he should not automatically select the type used by the club champion.

BASIC SUGGESTIONS

Most skilled players early in their careers adopt a definite way of attaining consistency. Some aim the ball to clear the net by a certain minimum height. Some aim at a specific spot on the table. Others play strictly by feel. None of these methods is necessarily better or worse for the budding champion. He should try them all and stay with the method that yields the best results. It does seem, however, that a combination of methods may be best— aiming for a certain minimum clearance on drives and chops, and for a precise spot for hard kills.

Skilled players also learn very early what can and what cannot be done with the opponent's various shots. Against any given shot there will be an optimum degree of spin that should be used, but the player should learn to what extent he can safely depart from this optimum. The racket angle and the arc of the stroke, including the hand action, can be similarly varied. The player should systematically study all these factors in order to improve his versatility.

A considerable amount of help along these lines can be obtained from advanced players, whose strokes and tactics can be analyzed and experimented with, and who may be able to explain why they play their strokes the way they do. Their comments, however, should always be compared with their actions. Many top players rely almost solely on "feel," never having broken down the various factors that have vaulted them into the upper ranks of the sport. Players of this type cannot be expected to be of much help.

Nevertheless, as much guidance as possible should be obtained from others. Ideally, this help should come from one of the coaches approved by the United States Table Tennis Association; they are listed in *Table Tennis Topics*, the Association's official periodical. If no coach is available, seek out someone with a keen analytical mind, who can communicate his ideas effectively, and who has great patience. Very few meet these qualifications and those who do are not all top players. Remember: a keen observer is infinitely better than a skilled player who cannot communicate.

The up-and-coming champion should attempt to play regularly against a veteran who has passed his peak. The old campaigner's game will remain relatively constant, so that these jousts should provide a good barometer with which to gauge the rising star's improvement. He should also play against those whose style is unorthodox and

bothersome. Many claim that this will ruin a player's
game, and there is a natural tendency to avoid it. On the
contrary, if that which is distasteful is constantly avoided,
it will stay distasteful, while the player who takes on all
comers will improve his tactics and enhance his versatility.

THE SERVE

The increased frictional quality and resiliency of sponge
have made it possible to apply more spin to the ball. The
service has therefore become once more a potent weapon,
and has helped to open up the game.

Straight chop and topspin services are quite effective,
but combinations of these spins with sidespin are much
more powerful. Every effort should be made to disguise
the amount of spin imparted to the serve. It is usually
impossible to gauge the amount of spin by watching the
ball itself. An opponent must therefore watch the movement of the racket applying this spin, so that he can to
some extent gauge the effect from the height of the racket
before and after the backswing and from its direction.
The less he is able to perceive this motion, the harder it
will be for him to estimate the amount of spin; he is then
more likely to make a weak return, and the service will
have provided initial control over the pattern of the play.
The server should therefore make his service stroke as
horizontal as possible and use as much hand action as
possible. Exaggerated body and arm motion will provide
added deception.

Both backhand and forehand services should be used
to provide variety. In doubles, however, the backhand
service is especially valuable for a righthander, since it
permits the server's partner to better position himself to
hit the receiver's return, commonly known as the "third
ball." A disadvantage of the backhand serve in doubles
is that the server is then out of position for his next stroke,

and must pay special attention to moving immediately to his neutral position (the position that maximizes his chances of returning any likely shot).

Although it is not necessary to describe the various services in this book, since they have been adequately covered elsewhere, one new one is so recent that it must be mentioned. It is quite controversial, and is being considered by the ITTF* at the time of this writing. It is quite possible that the wording of the service rule will be changed to outlaw this new serve; until that happens, however, it should be worth several points per game to an enterprising attacker.

This serve incorporates a very rapid, almost vertical racket swing. The racket starts at shoulder height, or higher, drops to just past the ball, and rises again immediately after passing it. Contact can be made on either the downward or the upward part of the stroke, thus imparting chop or topspin, either of which can be mixed with sidespin. Since the stroke is rapid, it is quite difficult for the opponent to discover which spin is present until the ball has been contacted. The receiver, therefore, has little more than a 50 per cent chance of making a good return, even if the spin is not severe. With good deception and severe spin, even the better players find the serve extremely difficult.

One should always serve with a definite purpose in mind. Do not serve just as a means of putting the ball in play. In addition to serving to force the opponent to make a particular type of return, one should practice serving to all parts of the table as a means of keeping him off balance. This same purpose can be furthered by varying the time taken between serves. In this connection, always think very deliberately about your service before

---

* The International Table Tennis Federation. This is the governing body of international table tennis; the USTTA is one of about 90 national associations affiliated with it.

you begin your motion; far too many players try to "quick-serve" the opposition, and end up by serving off the table or into the net. Vary the services as much as possible; not only will this give you an immediate advantage, but it will give you an insight into what opposing servers can do to you.

RETURN OF SERVICE

The return of the service is just as important as the service itself. In fact, it might be even more important, since it may nullify the potential strategic advantage for the server in addition to setting the stage for the receiver to gain control. Furthermore, most players generally have a few pet serves, which they rely on to gain points through set-ups; if these services are returned well, the receiver can often gain a significant psychological advantage.

The type of return depends on the receiver himself as well as on the serve. For example, a heavily chopped service may be driven, looped, or pushed back, depending on the receiver's capabilities and preferences with defense or attack. Similarly, the return of topspin may be by chop, block, or counterdrive. However, a given type of service should not always be returned in the same manner; e.g., don't always counterdrive a topspin serve. Such a routine permits the server to anticipate your return and thus gain a tactical advantage.

In order for the receiver to make the correct return, his body must be in the correct ("neutral") position. If he is equally capable with the backhand and the fore-hand, his right shoulder should be roughly in the middle of the possible serving angle. Actually, it will be a little to the left, since his reach is always greater on the fore-hand. If his forehand is the stronger side, as it is with most players, he will stand even more to the left. As always, he should be on his toes, with his knees and waist slightly flexed. This stance facilitates movement in any direction, and it is the beginning of the stroke position for any stroke. However, the receiver should be ready to jump, rather than stride, suddenly in any direction in case the service is entirely different from what was anticipated. He should be prepared for any service.

From the ready position, be prepared to move and *then* stroke. Even some of the better players make the mistake of standing straight up, flat-footed, and reaching instead of moving to the ball. In order to put you in the proper position for a good stroke, especially if that stroke is one that needs a long back-swing, the initial movement must be *rapid*.

The axiom that the eye should be on the ball is not true for the receiver during the service. Watch the racket while the ball is struck, and *then* watch the ball; the height to which the ball is thrown in service is quite immaterial. Since the ball must be tossed upwards vertically from an open palm, the toss can impart no significant spin. The spin is imparted by the racket. Furthermore, it is the direction and speed of the racket motion *at contact* that determines how much spin will be imparted to the ball. A last-minute change of racket motion can tremendously affect the imparted spin, and consequently the type of return that should be played. If the racket motion *at contact* is to the receiver's left, his return will tend to go toward the left, and vice versa. If the racket is descending at contact, then the serve will usually be some sort of chop, and conversely. It is therefore possible to recognize the spin on the ball and to take immediate corrective action—but only if all racket motion except that at contact is ignored.

Frequently, it is difficult to analyze the spin on a service, and some players will refuse to disclose what they are doing. If you find yourself in this kind of trouble, inquire of the player's teammates, or of others who have encountered him. It should be possible, eventually, to find out what spin was used and how. You should then practice the service yourself until you have mastered it.

Just as the service should be varied, so should the return. Constant use of the same return can result in disaster. An easy and effective return that has until recently been quite neglected is the half volley. It is especially effective against a fast topspin serve, and it can be placed well with little trouble. The half volley return is also useful against sidespin services, but a slow topspin return will usually provide more control. The slow and fairly high topspin return to the opponent's weaker side is often useful against almost any type of service.

FOOTWORK

Proper footwork is essential to one's balance and movement. The fundamental positioning of the feet for the various strokes is expounded in most table tennis books, but the manner of moving from one position to another is seldom covered adequately.

The knees should be flexed at all times. This will keep the body ready for rapid movement in any direction and will provide greater reach and improved balance. For the same reason, one should always stand on the balls of the feet.

As much as possible, one should move with short steps, since sudden long steps tend to impair the balance. It is, nevertheless, often necessary to cover large distances rapidly. Moving sideways is best accomplished by running, although for shorter distances the shuffling step of the fencer preserves better balance. To move backwards, however, a long jump should be used, usually preceded and followed by one or more short steps of adjustment; back-pedaling is useful if time permits. The opposite motions may be used when approaching to retrieve a drop shot.

Most players find it easier to maintain balance when moving toward the table rather than when moving away. This implies that the neutral position should be in general somewhat farther back than is commonly understood. The neutral position, which changes after every shot, is defined with respect to the possible angles to which the ball could be hit, rather than with respect to the table.

Footwork is frequently neglected by the pusher, and even some of the better players do not seem to consider foot movement necessary when pushing. It cannot be emphasized too much, however, that moving the body toward the line of flight of the ball will always give improved control. This is accomplished by moving the right foot on most pushes; this movement has the advantage that, if you are presented with a weak return, you will probably be in an ideal position for a backhand drive. That foot, however, must be moved back to the neutral position after each stroke in preparation for the next one; moving back gives the advantage of a slightly farther distance from the table which will give you an extra split second in which to handle a sudden drive.

Footwork should be practiced until it is second nature. Brilliant defensive shots are made despite, not because, the player is out of position.

GENERAL STRATEGY

The better player does not always win. He can and often does lose matches because of mental lapses. A player should therefore always be mentally alert throughout a match. Complete concentration is imperative.

Patience is also a valuable commodity in general strategy. It helps in locating an opponent's weakness, and it also helps to wear him down and tire him. The overall importance of patience, however, is that it gives you the necessary time to wait for the loose ball, i.e. a high ball or one with little spin, which will permit you to kill it or to mount an attack.

It is also important to look at the right thing at the right time. Any good player is constantly on the move in relation to the table. The table is stationary, however, and it should never be necessary to look at it. Watch the ball; the ball moves, but the table doesn't. It is quite easy to strike the ball and direct it to a specific part of the table without looking at that part in the least. But once the ball has been struck, further observation of it serves no purpose. Attention should then be turned to the opponent; watch his general movement and also that of his racket, his hand, and his arm. Transfer your attention back to the ball only after he hits it.

Sponge gives the advantage to the attacker. Sponge players should therefore avoid, if possible, falling back on defense, even when receiving. You may have to do so if your opponent's counterdrive is superior, or it may be tactically advantageous to defend if you are out of position or tired, or if you feel that it will adversely affect your opponent. Nevertheless, it pays to evolve a definite style of play—aggressive if you use sponge—and to force the opponent to play against that style as much as possible.

When playing in a tournament, it is always a good idea to practice on as many tables as possible in different parts of the hall. They may not all have the same bounce, so you may have to adjust your strokes and even your strategy. You can find out at the same time if one side of the hall has better lighting, so that you can use this information to advantage when your matches are called. It also pays to practice at the tournament site with a teammate; you know his style and the effect of his spin, so that you will be able to determine if it is the conditions, rather than your opponents, that cause any difference in your own play.

2/Attack

The most important aspect in attacking play is *touch*. It is essential to develop early the feel of a correctly driven ball, whether it be low or high, fast or slow. The racket angle will change on these various strokes, all of which should be practiced so that the different angles are selected automatically. At the same time, the speed variation that is possible on any shot should be studied, as should the permissible variation in placing. Good use of this information can be made to tire an opponent. But in all of these strokes, the *feel* should be cultivated. One should have the impression of carrying the ball over the net rather than banging it like a projectile; it seems to hang momentarily on the better player's racket. The arm motion should reach its maximum speed at the time of contact.

The backswing, contact, and follow-through should be integrated into one smooth, continuous motion, with no hesitation at any point. Although some better players use hardly any backswing, this practice is not recommended. It is true that a stroke with no backswing will permit more deception, but the improved rhythm, timing, balance, and control in the longer stroke far outweigh this advantage.

Backswing is important on all drives, but its importance is increased on the harder strokes. The harder the stroke, the longer the backswing and follow-through. The longest backswing is, of course, on the loop drive, with the fastest racket motion of them all. As the pace of a drive is increased, the more horizontal one's body and arm motion become. Conversely, one can stand more vertically and swing more vertically on easy drives. Again, the harder the drive, the more topspin becomes necessary, and the more the racket should be closed. At the same time, the stance should be more sideways, and the body should roll more with the stroke.

It is difficult to lay down hard and fast rules about the racket angle, as this depends to a considerable extent on the rubber and also on the opponent's spin. In general, the racket is closed on all drives, with all types of rubber. With pimpled rubber on very slow drives, however, it occasionally becomes necessary to have the racket vertical or slightly open, and an extremely stiff chop could also make such an angle a necessity.

All attackers should make a point of practicing the kill. Before the advent of sponge this was difficult to arrange, as it was difficult to return the kill with rubber. Good defenders can now do it with ease, especially if told where to expect the kill, so that now there is no excuse for all the missed kills that we see in tournaments.

TACTICS

Although one should practice these kills until they are second nature, the bread-and-butter shots are the medium speed drives. These are the major part of the hitter's game, and they should be fully exploited at all speeds, depths, and angles.

Body and hand action will help to lift stiff chops, although at the same time reducing the amount of control that a more simple arm motion would provide. Hard chops can also be lifted more readily if they are contacted much earlier than usual: a flat hit timed almost like a half volley is remarkably effective in this connection, and has the advantage of producing an unusual return that is difficult to handle, especially if the topspin that is reduced on a flat hit is replaced by a slight sidespin.

When driving to a chopper who suddenly counterdrives, one should not chop except as a last resort. There is usually too little time for this, and in any case it is undesirable to relinquish the attack just because of one "nuisance" shot. Instead, the sudden hit should be counterdriven if possible. If time does not permit a backswing, then the half volley should suffice.

THE BACKHAND DRIVE AGAINST CHOP

Most players have a weakness, and this is usually it. Nevertheless, although it is advisable to protect about two-thirds of the table with the forehand if this is your strong point, you will still be a better player if you have a good backhand drive.

As with most strokes, the harder this is played, the more sideways you should stand. Many excellent players stand quite square to the table for the backhand drive even when playing against chop; they thereby gain the advantage of an easier turn back to the forehand, but the square stance definitely restricts the backswing, the follow-through, and perhaps the attainable angles. The recommended procedure, therefore, is to turn more sideways, and to develop light footwork on the toes to ease the turn to the forehand.

Many players—perhaps most—change the grip for the backhand drive. By all means, move the thumb toward the center of the blade if you find that this provides more pressure and firmness to the stroke, but bear in mind that a sudden change to the forehand will need a correspondingly quick change in the grip. The more major grip changes, such as moving the fingers on the handle, are definitely to be eschewed.

As on the backhand chop, the elbow is normally held away from the body; it is essentially the fulcrum of the stroke. The forearm should rotate about this point in an

BACKHAND DRIVE

The use of two fingers on the blade for the backhand is quite unusual and considered unorthodox. The high ball allows for more of a forward follow-through than that used with a ball which bounces lower. The elbow is held free and forward of the body. The ball is struck more in front and forward of the body than with the forehand. The free and playing hands are synchronized to give control and speed. The racket is closed because the ball is higher than the net and a hard drive is executed. The arm is practically straight upon the completion of the follow-through. (Brooke Williams, top ranking player and U.S. World Team member)

arc, the inclination of which will naturally depend on the type of racket—more vertical for rubber, more forward for sponge. As much backswing as possible should be taken, and on very hard drives the stroke should be finished by extending the arm completely from the shoulder.

Since this stroke is fundamentally shorter than the corresponding stroke on the forehand, hand action is more useful to increase the speed and spin. This hand action should be in the same sense as the forearm action; i.e., the hand should pivot with the wrist as the fulcrum, and the plane of the resulting arc should be identical to the plane of the arc made by the arm. The hand will lag behind the arm until just before contact, when it will move forward, finishing in front of the arm just after contact.

At the end of a hard backhand drive, the racket will finish above shoulder height. Because the stroke is shorter than on the forehand, more *conscious* lift is required. Really hard drives, bordering on kills, are difficult and tiring for most players, and the player is rare indeed who can consistently hit hard from the backhand. Because of this, lobs are usually aimed to that side, and it will therefore pay you well to be able to kill them without having to run around them.

The Flick

The backhand flick is used to break up a pushing duel, or to cope with short, low chops. Like the half volley, it has no backswing. It does, however, have a follow-through, which should be as smooth as that of a drive. Especially with rubber, the blade should be tilted back so that the racket is half open, and it should be closed at the moment of contact. The fine timing necessary for this motion is extremely critical, and is undoubtedly the reason for the comparative rarity of good flickers. Many players use a type of flick instead of a backhand drive, but the shot is much easier when the ball is deep, as it usually is. Since topspin is applied by the hand action, the follow-through need not be as high as on a drive, and can be at shoulder height or even below.

FOREHAND DRIVE AGAINST CHOP

The forehand drive is the main point of most games. It is the shot that players are most willing to practice, as it should be. The grip for the forehand drive is essentially the same as that described in Chapter 1. The grip should be firmer than for a chop, and should be on the blade rather than the handle. The thumb should be low, but the forefinger can be higher on the blade depending on preference. A slight pressure should be applied by the forefinger.

The body position should usually be about one foot from the table, and at an angle to it that can vary from about 45 degrees for an easy drive to almost 90 degrees

for a hard one. Standing closer to the table will result
in lack of control over deep chops and vulnerability to
counterdrives, whereas a deeper stance will result in
unnecessary reaching.

On a medium drive, the backswing is usually to the
side of and about one foot behind the body. It will be
shorter for an easy drive, and longer for a harder one.
The medium drive is essentially a forearm shot; the racket
describes an ellipse, the lower end of which is roughly
level with the elbow about which the hand is pivoting.
The ellipse is inclined at some 30-60 degrees to the horizontal and is traced out in opposite senses depending on
the type of racket. For sponge, the racket moves along the
upper side of the ellipse and returns to its starting point
along the lower side; i.e., the hitting stroke can be con-

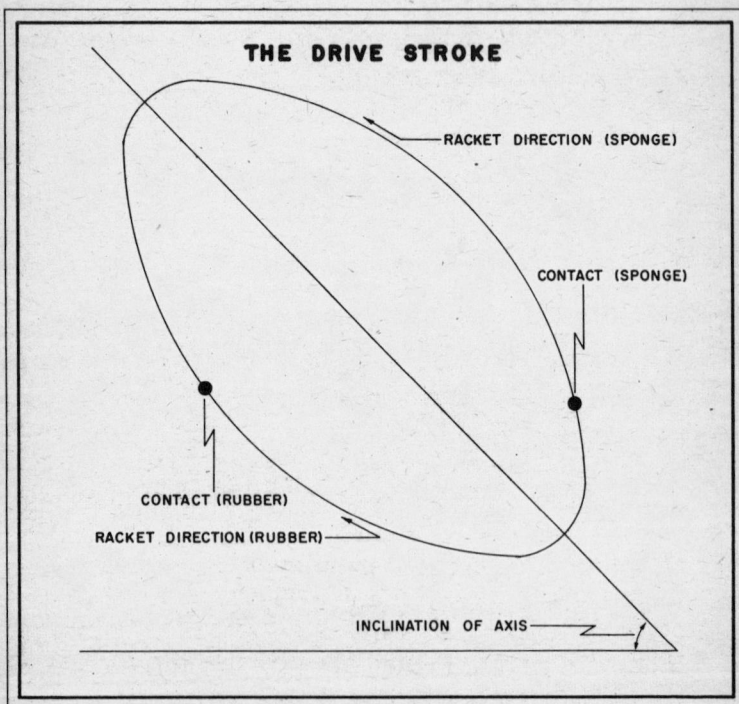

THE DRIVE STROKE

RACKET DIRECTION (SPONGE)

CONTACT (SPONGE)

CONTACT (RUBBER)

RACKET DIRECTION (RUBBER)

INCLINATION OF AXIS

sidered to move more vertically at the start, and more horizontally in the follow-through. With rubber the racket moves up the lower side of the ellipse, and returns down the upper side; this stroke can be considered to be more horizontal in the approach, and more vertical in the follow-through. If the ellipse is narrowed so that it is virtually a straight line, then this line will be more horizontal for sponge than for rubber. With either surface, the racket should usually be closed, more so with sponge than with rubber. Hitting in this way, above the horizontal diameter of the ball, gives a suitable amount of topspin and speed, combined with excellent control.

On harder drives, some hand action can be added. The blade will lag behind the line of the forearm during the approach, snapping forward at contact and moving ahead in the follow-through. The motion of the hand flows in the same direction as that of the arm. This hand action on drives, kills, and flicks should be tried only when one already has excellent consistency without it.

At what point of its trajectory should the ball be struck? At the maximum height, before, or after? The answer depends to a slight extent on the player's stage of development, and to a considerable extent on the type of drive. Beginners are better off hitting at the highest point of trajectory, since at this point the ball is moving neither up nor down. The better players, however, frequently hit earlier than this, while the ball is still rising. This permits a more forward motion, which adds more speed to the drive; but it demands more speed and quicker reflexes than the average beginner possesses. As you might deduce from this, the harder the drive, the earlier one is likely to make contact. Striking the ball after the height of bounce will produce more spin. These variations in contact time, however, are small compared to the one major departure from early hitting—the loop drive. This is described in more detail in a later section; it is sufficient

to point out here that the loop is made by contacting considerably *after* the height of bounce.

In the forehand drive, the elbow angle is appreciably greater than on the backhand, since more room is available. Whereas the elbow angle on the backhand is about 90 degrees, it is 120-140 degrees on the forehand. This puts the racket farther away from the body and adds more speed, although it permits possibly less deception than the backhand.

In the follow-through of a forehand drive, the body turns to face the table or, on harder drives, turns even farther. As the weight comes forward onto the front foot, which itself may have to be moved forward during a hard drive, the heel of the rear foot will leave the floor. Many players take this action farther and lift the rear foot completely from the floor as the front foot comes down.

The follow-through usually ends at about head height or higher and in front of or to the left of the head. This will vary considerably, however, depending on the type of drive being made. If the approaching ball is a heavy chop, for instance, the drive will be more vertical and the follow-through can be above the head or, with rubber, to the side and even behind it. On the other hand, the follow-through of a kill, which is a considerably more horizontal stroke, may never reach shoulder height; this stroke can actually have an overall downward motion, the follow-through ending near the table surface. The ex-

FOREHAND DRIVE AGAINST CHOP WITH SPONGE
Keeping the eyes on the ball throughout the stroke, short quick steps are taken to attain proper position. Waist is bent to assist in imparting topspin to the ball. The stroke is well to the side of the body, comes up and then forward with a closed racket. (This is contrary to the rubber racket stroke which comes forward and then up with the racket face either vertical or slightly open.) Slight hand motion is used in the same direction as the stroke. Body and weight are shifted upward and forward during the stroke. The left arm is used to help maintain balance. (Danny Pecora, former U.S. Junior Champion, and second ranked U.S. player)

FOREHAND DRIVE FOLLOW-THROUGH

The weight has been shifted from the rear foot to the forward foot. More speed and control would be obtained by bending the body slightly at the waist and by rotating the body in the direction of the stroke. The free arm aids balance. Two fingers on the blade is a frequent variation of the normal grip used by several of the better players. The conventional sidewards stance gives a longer stroke with more spin and control. (Brooke Williams, top ranking player and U.S. World Team member)

FOREHAND DRIVE AGAINST CHOP WITH RUBBER

The backswing is a bit higher and shorter than sponge backswing. Sidewards stance is achieved by body movement. The lagging and then upward racket sweep add hand movement. The racket stroke with rubber is almost straight up with a slightly open racket. If this stroke had been made with a sponge racket, the stroke would have been more forward with a closed racket, and the follow-through would have been forward of the head instead of directly above it. (Martin Reisman, former U.S. and Canadian Champion)

treme of this is the slap kill, like a hammer action, played on a high-bouncing ball near the net; hand action added to this motion provides extra power.

The addition of sidespin (by inclining the hand more toward the net) on medium drives adds to one's driving effectiveness without sacrificing accuracy. It also simplifies the drive against heavy chop.

From the preceding paragraphs on the drive, it is apparent that hand action is optional. There is no doubt, however, that controlled hand action in the direction of the forearm motion provides definite advantages, and virtually all the top players exploit it to the utmost. These advantages include speed, spin, controlled variation (and therefore deception), power, and margin for safety. The extra speed forces the opponent farther back, reducing the effectiveness of his counterdrives.

DRIVES AGAINST TOPSPIN

Before the days of sponge, it was difficult to counterdrive consistently, and the good counterdrivers were as talked about as good flickers. Sponge, however, in giving the attacking player the advantage, has also sharply altered the sport so that in many parts of the world virtually every shot except the service is a counterdrive. In the United States, the counterdrive is an integral part of the games of almost all the top players.

Even the term "counterdrive" itself has lost its meaning with the advent of sponge. Before sponge, a counterdrive by definition was a shot made by the defending player against his opponent's drive, and it was therefore always made at a distance from the table. Now, however, a rally may consist of ten or twenty counterdrives in a row. Some of these may be played from fifteen feet behind the table; some may be quite conventional drives from close to the table, differing from those described above only in that the racket and the stroke itself are sloped more acutely forward to overcome the approaching topspin; and some may be made so quickly that they have no backswing—they are half volleys, but more powerful half volleys than those normally made with rubber in that there is a well-controlled follow-through.

The principles of these various strokes are all identical: the foe's topspin must be overcome, and one's own topspin applied. Furthermore, since the whole idea behind counterdriving today is to maintain the attack and derive from it a more advantageous position, the most important factor in counterdriving is *speed*. On any shot, hitting hard and successfully contacting the other side of the table necessitates topspin. But when the opponent's shot already has its topspin, which is opposite to the topspin that you will apply, the effect is that much more topspin must be applied than on a normal drive against chop. The racket must therefore be much more *closed*. The tendency on counterdriving with sponge is to hit off the end of the table; it is therefore good to remember that if the racket is above the ball the ball cannot rise: keep the racket closed.

The correct racket angle can be acquired only by constant practice. It will be more horizontal the harder the drive and the harder the opponent's drive. The same applies to the direction of the stroke as a whole, but it is important that enough upward motion be used to provide, with the stroking action of the closed racket, the topspin necessary to bring the ball down. The racket must move upward and *then* forward.

During a counterdriving rally, both players will constantly be advancing and retreating to and from the table. Naturally, the harder one's opponent's drive, the farther one tends to retreat, confident that the opponent will find a drop shot against your hard drive almost impossible. Conversely, the weaker his drive, the closer your approach. The objective is to hit hard enough to force the opponent back. His shot will then be weaker in view of the greater distance that it must travel, and the power of your shot will also tend to force him to hit weakly, in order to preserve his control.

Counterdrives, in addition to being hard, should also be moved from side to side. If neither player errs on his stroke, the rally will continue until, in lawn tennis parlance, one makes a passing shot. This whole procedure is much quicker than a rally involving a chopper, and it is this type of play that has given rise to the recent concern over physical fitness. The legs, in particular, must be extremely limber and powerful.

In order to be able to cover the back court quickly, it is frequently necessary to make sudden moves in either direction. This can be done only from a wider stance than is usually employed in driving, since it is impossible to push off with a vertical leg.

It follows from the necessity of the wide stance that the forehand shot may well have to be made *while the player is much squarer to the table* than on a normal drive. Not only will the backhand stance be squarer to the table, but the ball will often be contacted more in front of the body than at the side.

The topspinner who is driven well back from the table may experience trouble in hitting hard and low, since from that distance he has very little margin for error. He therefore deliberately hits a good deal higher than on a normal drive, and applies more top spin, by stroking more vertically than on a closer counterdrive, to bring the ball down on the other side of the net. This extra topspin makes the ball even harder to hit, and the opponent must close his racket even more. All degrees of height and topspin are seen in this type of counterdrive, or "defensive drive," one extreme being the lob.

Hand action is quite useful in these strokes. Its effect

BACKHAND COUNTERDRIVE WITH SPONGE

Contrary to general belief, many penhold players possess very fine backhands. The closed racket is made possible by extending the racket to the side instead of being vertical, sideways forward bending from the waist, and the racket grip which removes the small and ring fingers from the blade. The follow-through is the same as the shakehand backhand, crossing in front of the face to the right and above the head. (Lee Dal Joon, South Korean Champion and tenth ranked player in the world) is to magnify the topspin applied by the conventional racket movement, so that it facilitates overcoming the opponent's spin and also makes your return more difficult to handle. It also permits you to make a reasonable shot while off balance and, if combined with sidespin by inclining the hand toward the table, gives bounces of varying heights.

THE DROP SHOT

The drop shot has been well described in many books, though its consideration has been limited to use against the chop. Against the chop, the shot should be practiced to counter returns of various heights, depths, and speeds. It will be found that short, low balls are best for effective drop shots, but more latitude is permissible when the opponent is well out of position.

In an all topspin game, opportunities for a drop shot are extremely rare, and when they are presented, the shot is very difficult. It requires a great amount of practice. The racket should be held loosely in the hand—more so than when dropping against a chop—and very closed, to prevent the topspin from taking the ball high. Since the tendency of the drop against topspin is to go deeper than against chop, there is little point in dropping near the centerline all the time, as is usual against chop, for the opponent will have a fairly easy time reaching it. Instead, the drop against topspin should be angled as much as possible away from the opponent. The resulting shot is very effective, usually resulting in a high return and occasionally in an immediate point.

THE LOOP DRIVE

The loop drive, or loop, the most recent stroke in the game, is feared because of the extreme amount of topspin. In the magnitude of this spin, the shot is quite unlike any other in table tennis or probably in any other ball game. Since the shot is so revolutionary, a brief history probably will help in its understanding.

The loop drive was introduced to U.S. tournament table tennis in 1955 by Mr. Bill Rapp, then of Detroit. As far as we have been able to determine, Rapp was the first serious exponent of the loop anywhere in the, world. In 1957, in the U.S. Open Championships in South Bend, the spotlight focused on Rapp's unorthodox stroke and overpowering topspin. Unranked, unseeded, and unheralded he annihilated the number three seed in the second round, in one of the great upsets of U.S. tournament history. Rapp won purely because of his loop drive; his subsequent early loss to a sound half-volley player showed, as was well known, that he was not of national caliber. Despite the sensation caused by Rapp's win, none of the better players gave serious attention to learning the new stroke. Since it was developed by a player of less than championship ability, it was no doubt considered an eccentric weapon.

The loop was rediscovered at the end of the decade, perhaps independently by the English in 1959 and the Japanese in 1960. The discovery this time was made by better players, and immediately it was recognized that the loop was the antidote to some of the purely defensive artists whose heavy chopping tactics were catching up with sponge drives.

It was another three years before the loop was accepted in the U.S. as the powerful instrument that it is. In early 1963, the United States Table Tennis Association invited Stanley Jacobson and Derek Baddeley, of England, to demonstrate the stroke to U.S. players. They did, and with it easily defeated every high-ranking American they faced in exhibitions and matches. By the time of the U.S. Open in Detroit several weeks later, however, Americans had learned to cope with the loop drive and were able to defeat the two Englishmen, but only after titanic struggles. Further practice against European teams enabled the United States to defeat England 5-3 in the Prague World Championships one month later.

The loop drive in its early form had a rather high trajectory, but subsequent development has lowered this so that it is barely higher than that of a normal drive. What distinguishes the two is that the loop drive has an *extreme* amount of topspin. Its amount can be judged from the fact that the best defensive player in the U.S. could not keep the ball within three feet of the table when he first faced Baddeley in 1963. The stroke is best learned by starting from well below the table surface with a racket blade that is just about vertical. The swing should also be vertical, and the follow-through above the head. This swing is extremely fast, with its maximum speed coming at the time of contact and increased optionally by means of hand action. The ball is contacted almost tangentially, so that the high speed of the racket is converted, on the ball, into rotation rather than forward motion. The ball travels fairly slowly, in a high loop, until it drops nearly vertically on the far side of the net. The intense spin then yields a low, forward bounce which drops rapidly. The unexpected acceleration as the spin bites into the table surface makes the return very difficult to control.

In the loop drive, the racket barely touches the ball in a skimming action that produces the maximum amount of spin. Too much contact gives a drive with heavy topspin, but not enough for a loop. It is quite difficult to learn to skim the ball in this way. The racket *must* be closed, and this adds to the difficulty. When the stroke is first learned, slight sidespin, added by cocking the hand forward toward the net, may help to avoid missing the ball completely, but the student should not rely on this sidespin too much; sidespin on the loop can detract from the amount of topspin.

The beginner should use the loop only against a chop or a push. He will have footwork trouble initially, since he must adopt a stance that is farther from the ball (to produce more spin with a more extended arm) and farther back from the table (so that the ball is descending) than on a drive. He will find it best to learn with balls bouncing somewhere in the middle of his half-court, but eventually the footwork must be developed so that long and short balls also can be handled. Furthermore, since the backhand loop is more difficult and less effective, the student must be very agile so that he can cover more of the table with the forehand. After looping, if the next ball can be killed, then he must still be on his toes in order to quickly approach from his loop position to be closer to the table.

In executing this form of the loop drive, the ball should be contacted after the height of bounce and about even with the right shoulder. The shoulder will move upward and somewhat forward during the stroke, adding more speed to the racket. The body motion is from the waist.

The faster loop, developed only in the last two or three years and hardly exploited yet in this country, starts at about table level. The racket angle and the direction of the swing are both much more horizontal, and the body is inclined much more forward than on the slow loop; the overall effect on a spectator is much like that of a kill of a fairly low ball, even though the ball is only skimmed. The follow-through is also much like that of a kill: forward of the head, which is at that time only about two feet or so from the table surface. This stroke combines almost all of the spin of the slow loop with much of the speed of a drive. It is extremely difficult to execute, more so even than the slow loop, but as might be expected, it has led to further developments. A player who has command of both strokes can also perform anything in between, with the result that most of his drives are converted into semi-loops. The top players use much of this action now against balls that have topspin, whereas the shot was developed originally as a means of hitting chop.

The loop drive cannot be performed with a pimpled rubber racket, because it is impossible to impart enough spin to the ball. With a considerable amount of practice a fair loop may be performed with a regular sandwich racket. However, since much more spin may be facilitated by the use of inverted sandwich, that is the racket used by the great majority of attacking players. It is recommended that the loop drive be attempted with inverted sandwich only.

FOREHAND LOOP WITH INVERTED SPONGE
The speed of the stroke is evidenced by the racket appearing out of focus in the second and third photos and that only three sequence frames are used for the entire stroke. On the backswing the body is bent and the hand extended down as low as is practical to assure the long stroke necessary to obtain the maximum racket speed. The racket face is closed throughout the stroke. Hand action, straightening of the body, elbow and shoulder movement all help to give the maximum speed to a racket which is just barely skimming the ball. Despite the extreme racket speed the ball is still seen in the third frame, thus indicating relatively slow ball speed but tremendous topspin. The left-hand movement has aided balance. Slight sidespin has assisted ball control. (Dell Sweeris, third ranked U.S. player and World Team Member)

The loop drive is virtually guaranteed to break up a pushing game. At one time it was also guaranteed to force the defender to return a set-up and to gain an outright winner even against heavy chop. Today, however, although most players have learned not to give their opponents many opportunities to loop, most have also learned to return the loop fairly well when necessary. Nevertheless, it is still extremely difficult for the pure defender to defeat a good player who combines the loop with the normal drive and the kill. There are only two defenders on the world men's ranking list. The loop is so effective that all but the very best defenders must at some time or other either contend with the kill or else resort to the half volley, the counter drive—or attack!

Any return against the loop requires a good deal of practice, since the extreme amount of topspin makes it only too easy to hit off the table. Furthermore, it is difficult to return the ball with speed—almost the only way to prevent further aggression—since a fast stroke must have topspin, which is difficult to apply in the face of the already existing spin. The best defenders use chop against the loop, either from a distance where the very low ball can be struck almost horizontally, or from quite close where the stroke must be almost vertical and rapid. Attackers, however, being normally closer to the table, usually block with very closed rackets, often held loosely, or else they counterdrive if the loop rises high enough; sidespin may be used on this counterdrive. These shots tend to be more effective than the chop, since the longer stroke of the loop does not mesh so well with the quick response needed to handle a drive or a block. In addition, the chop return gives the looper a further chance to loop, whereas a block or a drive does not.

3/The Push

The push, or chop of a chop, can be considered to be intermediate between attack and defense. More correctly, it is a vital part of both types of game. Either way, it deserves a short chapter to itself.

TECHNIQUE AND TACTICS

We begin with a reminder that one of the most important and yet neglected aspects of the push is the footwork. This has already been covered in Chapter 1. As in any other footwork, that for the push should be practiced until it is second nature.

Another source of error in the push is the all-too-common effort to load up the spin. Rather than trying to chop every push heavily, the player should attempt to vary the spin constantly. On no account should he try to outspin his opponent unless he knows that his own spin is the more powerful and consistent; spin should be intensified to one's own ability, not to that of an opponent. More sidespin is employed in pushing than is usual in longer-range backspin strokes; this is accomplished by bending the wrist so that the racket is inclined towards the net from the wrist. This position is not varied during the stroke, unlike conventional hand action, which is a common feature of the push.

On the push the ball is usually contacted well after the height of its trajectory, thus giving improved consistency. For speed variation, however, and also for change of direction if a sharp angle is needed, contact can be made before the height of bounce; in this case, it will be important that the racket be less open than when contact is made with a descending ball.

As in longer-range chopping, it will be necessary to compromise with the depth of the shot. If the other player is likely to push the return, then one's stroke should be deep. This will minimize the possibility of a sharply angled response, and will make it more difficult for the opponent to keep his own push low. Furthermore, your deep push can afford to be higher than normal, in the interest of accuracy, since you have a fraction of a second longer to react to a sudden hard return.

If the opponent is a good looper, however, or even if he drives well from deep chops, it is better for the push to be shorter. It can, of course, be deep to the backhand if, like most players, the opponent is weaker on that side.

Another factor in one's choice of depth is the opponent's ability to flick: depth will minimize this risk. If he does flick, however, the normal reply should be the half volley, unless the flick is slow enough to permit the backswing necessary for a drive. The half volley on the forehand is an especially valuable stroke in this connection, since it is so rare; when pushing, the body and arm positions are far better suited to backhand shots and for counterdrive or chop, so that the forehand half volley is seldom expected. Unfortunately, in the United States at least, it is also seldom encountered.

Although considerations such as the above may dictate that the push should be aimed, e.g., deep, its depth should always be varied randomly as should its position between the sidelines. Most pushes should go where they do least harm, but the pusher should never permit his opponent to get set.

A final source of error is too short a follow-through. Follow-through—towards the net, not across the body—

BACKHAND PUSH WITH SPONGE

Body is to the side with the left foot away from the table. Backswing is about waist high and maintains the same approximate height throughout the stroke. Absolutely no wrist is used. Eyes remain on the ball throughout the stroke. Contact with the ball is made to the side of the body. Follow-through is continued until the racket is on the opposite side of the body with the arm fully extended and the elbow straight. There is a slight upward lift in the sponge follow-through that is not used with the rubber racket stroke. (Alice Green, high ranking U.S. girl)

FOREHAND PUSH WITH SPONGE

Basically this is the same as the backhand push except that a more sideward stance is required in order to execute the forehand stroke more to the side. (Alice Green, high ranking U.S. girl)

will give added control of direction and also of height. Short, punching pushes lead to generally erratic play, and often present the opponent with easy kills.

ATTACK AGAINST THE PUSH

It is most desirable to end a pushing duel by mounting an attack. Yet the sudden execution of a sharp drive is quite difficult. One's position is usually not suited to a drive; the opponent's push has a more varied spin than a normal chop; less time is available to make the necessary adjustments; and different muscles are suddenly brought into play. Yet one nevertheless must drive, particularly when the expedite rule is in force.

One solution to this problem is to use the stroke that can be made most nearly from the same position as the push—the flick. It must be remembered that, when flicking against a push, more lift is needed than against a normal chop; the ball often has more backspin, and the table prevents a low backswing. A very full follow-through will help to overcome the lack of backswing. Sponge also helps. With sponge rubber, the racket can be closed throughout the stroke, with no danger that the ball will hit the net. With rubber, however, it is usually necessary to begin the stroke with an open racket, which is rolled over the ball and thereby closed during contact; this motion calls for perfect timing—possibly the reason why there has been only one person who could flick consistently (Victor Barna).

If the flick or drive is returned with a good half volley, caution will be necessary on the second drive. The half-volley return after a stroke with little or no backswing is often almost dead; when driven, it therefore tends to hit the net, and when pushed it may clear the table completely. If this half volley is driven, the direction should be changed, so that the opponent cannot "dig in" with his half volleys.

4/Defense

Although the predominant trend in table tennis today is to an aggressive game, there will always be some players who prefer the more passive role. Furthermore, even the all-out attacker occasionally finds himself at a marked disadvantage, and he may have to fall back on the type of game normally considered to be defensive.

TACTICS

When faced by a player with a more aggressive or powerful game, one should always make good use of varied spins, in order to upset the opponent's timing as much as possible. One of the most effective spin shots is the service. The service, however, is used largely as a method of mounting an attack, so that it follows that even a defender should be able to hit the "third ball"— the shot after the receiver's return. The entire repertoire of services should be tested early in the match, so that the more effective ones can be capitalized on when the match reaches a crucial stage. The return of service should also be varied. The half-volley return is normally considered to be an attacker's weapon. Attack, however, is often the best form of defense, and a judicious use of half volleys can upset an opponent's timing perhaps more than anything else.

The neutral position should be well selected, this being much more important for the defender than the attacker, who has much more time in which to move. A player with a strong forehand should protect about two-thirds of the table with that side, which means that the neutral position for most players will be to the left. It should also be as near to the table as possible, allowance having been made for the greater ease of moving forward than backward. The quicker returns from a short defense are a further disruptive influence on the attacker's timing, and their effect can be augmented by admixture with occasional half volleys and counterdrives. (It is an extremely poor defender who cannot occasionally resort to attack, either purposefully or merely to dispatch a loose ball.) The half volley is especially good if the attacker expects a chopped return from his loop drive. It is also a good means of returning a sudden drive to the opposite wing, when the defender has insufficient time in which to make the necessary foot movements for a deep chop. This latter point is especially true on the backhand; the forehand half volley is a rather neglected, although potent, weapon that should be mastered.

The short-range defense requires a good deal of practice, as it permits the defender less reaction time. It usually demands a much more open racket than the long-range stroke, resulting in a smaller margin for error; this is sometimes compensated for by a "shoveling" type of swing, with more or less horizontal hand action at impact. Although this type of defense is much more demanding than the long-range version, it is definitely more difficult to attack against, and the defender is nearer the table for any opportunities that may be offered to kill.

In defense it is always necessary to compromise between short returns, to reduce the ease of driving and looping, and long returns to reduce angles. The close defense is less troubled by angled drives, yet is quite vulnerable to the very powerful drive that a deep chop permits; the short-range defender should therefore chop short. The longer-range defender, however, is in exactly the opposite situation; he is not troubled by hard drives, being very familiar with them, but he is in dire trouble if he permits his opponent to angle him. Deep chops are therefore essential for the long-range man; even at the expense of permitting the attacker to loop.

The long-range defender may also permit himself the luxury of returning his chops higher than the short-range player. He must do this, in fact, in order to give himself the necessary greater margin for error on the longer trajectory; furthermore, the added height will minimize the effect of the drop shot.

To summarize the last few paragraphs, the deeper defense permits an easier return of the drive, but has several disadvantages:

The counterdrive is less effective from further away.

The opponent's drop shot is more effective.

The defender's returns are higher.

His spin is less effective from farther away.

The attacker has more opportunity to angle.

The attacker has more time to cover his weak wing and to make up for any deficiency in his footwork. The conclusion therefore has to be in favor of the short defense.

Even a short-range defender can be angled if his placement is particularly poor. In returning short balls, he can minimize this possibility by aiming for the center of the table, for the opponent's body, or for his weak point. Such aiming is more effective when the defender is close to the table. It can force the attacker to slow down his game or to make errors, and it therefore gives the defender more opportunity to play a disruptive counterdrive.

The shorter the defense, the more spin that can be employed. Hand action is always more effective when close to the table, and it yields more spin against weak drives. In fact, as a general rule, the closer the defender stands, the more he uses the lower arm, from the elbow

to the wrist, and the less he uses his shoulder. His near-
ness to the table also permits him a greater use of sidespin, always a valuable adjunct to a chop. The farther
he retreats, the more he must turn sideways to the ball,
and the less he can use sidespin.

Nevertheless, all defenders are occasionally forced deep.
The primary objective then becomes the returning of the
ball. The secondary objective, as on every shot in the
repertoire, is the variation of spin. As a general rule, no
two consecutive chops should ever have the same amount
of backspin. The defender who permits his opponent to
get used to his spin strengthens the opposition; the one
who varies his spin can slow down his opponent, and
make him play with caution and timidity.

The advantage of the short-range defense is a relative
one. The choice of distance from the table will vary from
player to player, dependent on their reflexes and retriev-
ing ability, and also of course depending on the speed
of the ball. A player may deliberately choose to defend
deep because of one advantage that this permits: if he
is a sponge defender, or a sponge attacker temporarily
on the defensive, he can lob. This stroke has been used
by only a few players in the United States, largely because many clubs have low ceilings. The lob is a valuable
weapon if played well. For instance, it should be directed
to the attacker's weak side, usually his backhand, and
it should invariably be aimed deep; a short lob permits
the attacker to kill with an unretrievable angle. The
stroke on the lob is very similar to that on the loop drive
in that the racket should normally be vertical or slightly
closed; this, with hand action, permits the lobber to use
intense topspin, or a mixture of it with sidespin. Such
mixtures should be constantly varied.

When a defender chops very hard and low, he should
usually move closer to the table, since this ball is more
difficult to drive hard. If it is looped, the defender is then

in position to block. If it is not, he will be in position to
counterdrive what will probably be a weak drive. The
counterdrive should be aimed at the forehand, since the
opponent will have little choice other than to block, and
the forehand block is a rare stroke. If the opponent tries
to drive, he needs a longer arm stroke on the forehand
than on the backhand. If he does drive, then his backhand
becomes quite vulnerable to a second counterdrive from
the "defender."

TOURNAMENT TECHNIQUES

For a defender, the first goal should be to determine
the reaction of the opponent to all types of returns, including light and heavy chops, relatively high returns to
both sides, and counterdrives. Many better players, for
instance, have amazing trouble with "sitters" and err
when attempting to kill them, especially if the spin is
constantly varied.

It is also surprising that even some top players resort
to stereotyped tactics: a drop shot after the second drive;
driving the opponent's third serve; putting every third
drive down the line; looping two and then driving. All
players should study the others in their tournament brack-
ets to see if they are guilty of such habits.

A common error of defenders is trying to make the
opponent drive into the net; only the gifted few, with
heavy, low, consistent chops can afford this luxury. Even
the best chop can be handled by a strong hitter, and it
should not be discouraging if one's heaviest effort is returned hard. Persevere! The hitter's timing may suddenly fail him, or overconfidence may lead him into errors.
If your repertoire does include a stiff, low chop, this
weapon should be surreptitiously blended with other returns of varied height and spin, including the "nothing"
ball. The low, short chop should be avoided on long-

range defense as we said above; it is too easy to flick or drop shot.

It pays to give special attention to the way an opponent uses the drop shot. How often does he use it? Is it primarily a backhand shot or a forehand? His style of play may well vary from opponent to opponent, but his use of the drop shot probably will not.

When he does drop shot, you should return it with the backhand if possible. This permits you to flick or push, yet still leaves you in position for a half volley or counter-drive on the next shot—which is usually the most difficult shot in the game.

Try varying the return of the kill in order to prevent your opponent from getting set for a second kill. The long-range chop can be mixed with the high topspin lob for this purpose. The efficiency of the opponent's loop drive may govern your choice of frequency of lobbing.

In this connection, be sure to determine which wing is weak—and it may vary depending on the shot. Many players, especially in the United States, have weak backhands, and tend to run around the ball to play the forehand. Lobs should therefore be directed as much as possible to this weak side; the backhand kill is usually even weaker than the backhand drive.

CHOP

Since the chop is the usual basis of a defensive game, it will be treated in some detail, beginning with the first principles. The grip, for instance, is usually looser on defense than when attacking, and the thumb and index finger can often be lower on the blade. Many good defenders do not make these adjustments, which if used can deaden the blade sufficiently to permit increased control.

In a typical chop, most of the spin is imparted by the

forearm. It is therefore important, especially in the initial stages of learning to chop, to make a point of swinging the forearm rather than making a full stroke from the shoulder. The chopper should move early into a position in which the lower arm can swing comfortably under the ball without having to reach for it. *He should not use hand action* to add to the spin until his coach approves, and then only under the latter's expert supervision. Hand action is one extra complication, which will make it more difficult to learn control.

The point of contact with the ball—whether directly underneath, or somewhat to one side or the other—is a governing factor in the direction of the return. The chopper should consciously select the point on the ball at which he intends to make contact, and thereby derive a greater feeling of control.

The technique of varying the amount of spin applied in a chop should be learned as soon as consistency has been acquired. With pimpled rubber, the more vertical swing applied the more chop, whereas with sponge the stronger backspin is imparted by contacting the ball farther underneath, i.e., by swinging more forward. When hand action is eventually used, it will be found that these effects can be achieved readily, while hardly changing the arm motion. Either way, *the chop should be varied;* do not chop with a constant amount of backspin against a steady attack.

The amount of backspin applied is also a function of the amount of topspin on the approaching drive. The racket angle and the slope of the arm swing will therefore vary with the speed of the drive and its spin. A hard drive, which almost by definition will have a considerable amount of topspin, will generally be struck with a more vertical motion than an easy drive, the angle being of course governed by the type of racket surface used.

The amount of spin applied should always be within

FOREHAND CHOP WITH RUBBER

Since this player stays reasonably close to the table, the stance is more square to the table than most. Sidewards body movement replaces footwork, even though this is not generally recommended. The back-swing is fairly high (somewhat higher than it would be when using sponge), near the right shoulder. The stroke is almost straight down (as opposed to the more horizontal stroke with sponge), but the follow-through is across the body and at the finish of the stroke has an upward motion. There is a completely relaxed body and stroke. The hand motion in the same direction as the stroke is evident just before and after ball contact. (Martin Reisman, former U.S. and Canadian Champion)

BACKHAND CHOP WITH RUBBER

Adaptable anticipation has placed the player in the proper position. Classic footwork places the feet at a forty-five degree angle to the table. The stroke is almost straight down with the follow-through until the arm is straight and across the body, Slight hand action adds to the spin effectiveness. Weight shift from the rear to the forward foot is noted by foot movement and raising of the left heel. (Martin Reisman, former U.S. and Canadian Champion)

FOREHAND CHOP WITH RUBBER

Position is taken before the ball arrives, not during the time it has already arrived. Backswing is between elbow and shoulder well to the side. Elbow and shoulder do most of the work with slight hand movement in same direction as stroke during contact. Follow-through is made almost straight down with rubber, and not completed until the arm is straight. Weight is on rear foot on contact, shifting forward with body movement during contact. At contact the ball is lower than the table level, requiring bending at the waist which gets eye closer to the ball, thus slowing up relative movement. (Violetta Nesukaitus, current U.S. and Canadian Women's Champion) the control of the chopper. The use of too much spin, applied by stroking too vertically with rubber, will often send the chop into the net; too little forward motion with sponge will act in the same way. Conversely, swinging under the ball too much in an attempt to load the spin may present the opponent with a set-up; either striking timidly with the racket or by having insufficient downward follow-through with rubber will produce the same effect.

The player who tends to lose control of his chops will do well to pay special attention to his backswing and follow-through. Both should be combined in one smooth motion, whose maximum speed coincides with contact with the ball. The player should strive to get the feeling of holding the ball on the racket during the chop, since this will add to his control. A long follow-through will further this feeling, while a short, punching stroke will eliminate control and touch completely. Against a hard drive to the forehand, .this long stroke will start about shoulder height, and the follow-through will take the racket to a point in line between the left knee and the center of the table—with the arm outstretched.

STANCE

As with almost all strokes, the chop is best played with the knees flexed and the body inclined forward toward the ball. The use of small steps to get into position will not only preserve the balance, but will also enable this stance to be maintained.

As the body is inclined, the head can be lowered to bring it more nearly behind the oncoming ball. This action reduces the relative motion of the ball with respect to the eyes, permitting greater accuracy in stroking. It also forces the player to adopt an improved stance, and makes him turn more sideways.

FOREHAND CHOP WITH SPONGE

Using excellent anticipation the neutral position has placed him ready to stroke. The deep waist bend and low head tends to slow up the relative motion of ball and racket. Feet are in the ideal position at about a forty-five degree angle to the table. The sponge backswing is lower and the follow-through more horizontal than with rubber. (Mike Ralston, former U.S. Junior Champion and second ranked U.S. player)

Because of the physical differences between forehand and backhand strokes, many top players habitually take forehand chops from hard drives farther away from the table than those on the backhand. The forehand chops are therefore taken nearer to the floor. The racket must be swung more underneath the ball to lift it, and the chop is therefore heavier on the forehand.

HAND ACTION

The maximum control over one's chops is achieved by keeping the wrist firm in all directions. Nevertheless, it is often necessary to compromise with control in order to produce other effects. Accordingly, the wrist can be bent in one of two ways: First, if the arm is stretched out parallel to the net, with the racket blade vertical, then the hand can be bent toward the net or away from it. This motion is never made during the stroke. The racket occasionally may be held at some angle of this sort, however, when it is desired to add sidespin to a chop or push. Since the hand is not moved relative to the arm during the stroke, very little control is lost, although most players find that a good deal of practice is necessary before the chop can be precisely directed with and without this wrist angle.

The other wrist motion is at right angles to this first type. With the arm and hand as described above, the hand can be bent upward—away from the floor—or downward. This motion, termed in this book "hand action," is timed to coincide with contact; this aspect of timing is the reason for the reduced control in a shot with hand action. Ideally, at the time of contact, the hand and racket should be in exactly the same positions as they would be if the wrist were firm, except that they are now moving faster than before. To produce the desired effect, it is unnecessary to swing the hand to its fullest extent, which will inevitably result in further loss of control; this motion will seldom move the tip of the index finger more than about two inches. Occasionally a player seems born with hand action; his chops have a fluid "wrist" automatically. Usually, however, hand action will require a considerable amount of practice, especially if its extent is to be varied—as it must be to maximize its effectiveness.

CHOP AGAINST A HARD DRIVE

The conventional course of action against a hard drive is to retreat, in order to permit the ball and its spin to slow down, and then to chop hard with a firm wrist. The harder the drive, the more pronounced both the retreat and the chop must be in order to counteract it. At the same time, the harder the drive, the more sideways one's

position should be, to permit taking a longer stroke; the longer, full stroke is especially important when the on-coming drive is fast.

BACKHAND CHOP WITH SPONGE

The neutral ready position is taken well before ball arrival. A more sidewards stance is taken for the backhand chop than for the forehand, as is customary with better players. The backswing is at elbow level, somewhat lower than the backswing rubber players employ. As with the forehand sponge chop, the stroke is much more horizontal than with a rubber racket chop. No hand action is used. The follow-through is finished with a slight racket lift and the arm fully extended across the body. As with better players, the waist is not bent as much on the backhand chop as it is with the forehand chop. (Jack Howard, top ranking U.S. player and World Team Squad outstanding player in 1966)

It would seem logical from the foregoing that the kill should be returned with the longest possible stroke. The very nature of the kill, however, often precludes this luxury: time will not permit the longer stroke, and a shorter motion must be made. To maintain control on this shorter stroke, it will usually be necessary to attempt less backspin, to relax the grip somewhat, and to aim higher. The "flat" kill—the kill made by moving an almost vertical racket horizontally, relying for its topspin on the chop already on the ball—has less topspin than the conventional kill, and can be returned with less chop. All kills can be returned by lobbing. The half volley is another useful method which, however, demands the fastest of reflexes.

If possible, one should chop with more forward motion on the ball against a hard hitter. This will give him less time and decrease his margin for error. Against the *steady* hitter, however, it pays to slow down the defense in order to improve one's own steadiness.

THE BACKHAND CHOP

Just as the backhand drive is often the attacker's weak point, so is the backhand chop very often the Achilles heel of the defender. It therefore needs special treatment.

It is important to have the racket elbow well clear of the body on the backhand chop, which usually means lifting it somewhat. On the follow-through, this arm should be swung well across the body until it is almost outstretched and pointing to the right. Even so, this will usually be a shorter stroke than on the forehand because of the body's physical characteristics.

On a deep backhand chop—more so than on the forehand—the shoulders should be almost perpendicular to the net. Length is imparted to the stroke by beginning the backswing quite near to the left shoulder.

FOREHAND CHOP WITH SPONGE

Warmup jacket and trousers are worn. This is common practice by the better players prior to a match. During a tournament most top players wear shorts for freedom of movement. The position is taken well before the ball arrives. The left hand aids balance. The stance is squarer to the table and the feet wider apart than usual. The backswing is to elbow height and the stroke is almost horizontal; this is contrary to the high backswing and almost vertical stroke of the rubber player. The ball is contacted below table level to allow it to slow down and assist in making a low return. There is no hand action. The follow-through is completed by an upward motion to the left of the body. The eyes are on the ball throughout the stroke, and the waist bending makes the eyes closer to the ball at contact. (Jack Howard, top ranking U.S. player and World Team Squad outstanding player in 1966)

Unless sidespin is to be added, the racket and wrist should be held straight out just as on any conventional shot. Occasionally a good defender may hold his racket slightly forward of the wrist during a forehand chop, but on the backhand this will almost always result in loss of control. If sidespin is to be added, the racket and hand should be inclined somewhat toward the net—but this angle, too, should be held constant during the stroke. This sidespin on the backhand chop will help to bring a wide ball back to the table, helping to overcome the lack of reach on that wing.

A further result of one's different physical characteristics when playing a ball on the left with the right hand is that, as mentioned earlier, it is often played closer to the net. The stroke is commonly played with a less open racket than the forehand chop.

Many players cross the right leg over the left when playing chops wide on the backhand. This footwork is stylish and beautiful to watch, but has the disadvantage that it makes it extremely difficult to return to position. It should be avoided whenever possible.

THE LOB

The innovation of sponge has caused the offensive game to become more predominant by the inclusion of more effective serves, spin, and speed, as well as the introduction of the loop. So also has sponge helped the defensive tactics of the offensive and defensive player by adding a different stroke—the lob. The lob is a very high shot with a considerable amount of topspin, varied occasionally with sidespin. It is used primarily as a defensive weapon against the hard drive or kill.

The lob may be used with a rubber racket. However, its effectiveness is reduced almost to nil since the amount of spin imparted by a rubber racket is not nearly so much

as sponge spin. The high lob return with considerable spin can cause trouble to some of the best players unless they are used to playing against it. The extra height of the lob causes the opponent to reach far higher than is normal. So the drive of a lob is in itself a new stroke introduced by the sponge play of today. The height of the bounce causes the drive of a lob to be more downward and have less forward speed than the drive of a normal high ball. Thus, the defensive player has ample time to get to the drive and return it (on many occasions) with another lob, a chop, or even with an all out hard drive of his own delivered from ten feet or more from the table.

It may seem strange intentionally to hit a ball quite high. However, the height itself as well as spin can cause considerable trouble. The lob is not used except when

BACKHAND CHOP WITH SPONGE

Position is taken before the ball arrives. Backswing is slightly above the elbow, almost directly in front of the body. Elbow does most of the work with no wrist movement during contact. Follow-through is made almost horizontal and is completed with the arm straight on the opposite side of the body. The feet are perpendicular to the table. There is only slight weight shift. Contact is made with the ball at table height. Left arm helps maintain balance.

Points considered faults are: backswing is a bit too high for sponge; sponge backswing should be somewhat lower than with rubber. Ball contact should be made slightly to the side rather than in front of the body; a stroke in front of the body is generally harder to control and keep low. Ball should be contacted lower, waist bent more, and head closer to the ball; this is necessary to keep the return low, reduce relative motion of eyes with the ball and to facilitate stroking action to the ball to obtain adequate backspin. Right foot should be more to the player's right and weight shift from rear to forward foot should be more pronounced; this movement will give better balance and assist with the follow-through, thus giving more ball control. (Alice Green, high ranking U.S. Girl)

BACKHAND CHOP WITH RUBBER

Position is taken as the ball arrives. Backswing is slightly above the elbow, hand extended only slightly to the side. Elbow does most of the work with no hand movement during contact. Follow-through is made almost straight down and is completed with the arm straight and on the opposite side of the body. Leg crossover is necessary since the ball is well to one side of the table. Lifting of the right heel shows that weight has been shifted, with body movement, from the rear to the forward foot. At contact the ball is lower than table level but not as low as the forehand chop contact. (Violetta Nesukaitus, current U.S. and Canadian Women's Champion)

forced away from the table by a hard drive which would otherwise be missed or the return would be a set-up. The normal high-chopped return can be readily killed by the average tournament player since the bounce and spin are easily recognized at a comfortable height. The high chop may be hit quite flat, thus giving more speed to the drive; the chop underspin keeps the ball from sailing clear of the table. However, the high topspin avoids the flat kill since the racket must be well closed and the stroke much more downward than forward. In addition, the high chop bounce will be closer to the net than the top-spin which continues in the direction of flight. Thus, the racket and ball contact will be farther from the net on the drive of a lob than for a drive of a chop. This greater distance from the net often impairs the hitter's accuracy and reduces the possible angles at which the ball can be struck to the other side of the table.

The execution of the lob is somewhat similar to that of the loop. The ball is contacted well after the height of the bounce. A long stroke is used, starting at about knee level and following through well over the head. The ball is brushed as much as is practicable rather than hit, so that the maximum spin is imparted. The racket blade is vertical or closed; an open racket will produce much less spin, thereby making it possible for the lob to be angled and killed more readily. With practice the degree of topspin and sidespin can be varied, thus keeping the offensive player from getting set. High lobs are much more effective to the opponent's backhand, since relatively few players can hit a high backhand very hard. The lobber should always be on the alert for a timid drive, since this is the ball he should counterdrive hard in order to win the point.

The player who finds himself facing a high lob for the first time will make far more errors than he feels he should. He often becomes frustrated in his attempts to kill every ball, and then loses many points because of his own agitation. About the only way to learn to hit a lob consistently hard is by a great amount of practice against the lob. However, hard drives against a lob for long periods of time may cause arm strain. Practice a while and then rest. Since the less time the ball makes contact with the racket the less time there is for the opponent's spin to take effect, the lob drive should be hit hard or a drop shot used. As with the drop shot against the chop, the drop shot stroke should be camouflaged as much as possible, particularly since the drop against a lob will bounce clear of the table. Since the lobber will be able to get back most hard balls driven to him and since he is waiting on a timid drive to kill, it is essential that the offensive player vary the angle and speed of his drive. Even an occasional chop drive may be effective, particularly if the lobber does not have a good drive.

5/Preparation for Tournament Play

For one who will be playing matches in a major tournament from morning to night over a two or three day period—or even for two weeks if you are fortunate enough to represent your country in the World Championships—proper mental and physical preparation is an absolute necessity. There is, however, no generally accepted basic training routine for table tennis; many top-notch players vary considerably in the amount and type of training that they employ, many preferring to work out their own methods in accordance with their individual needs. Furthermore, there is much more to physical condition than just training. For these reasons, this chapter will provide only guidance and the minimum requirements. Suggestions for further reading are given in the Appendix.

CONDITIONING

Although many top players do not train or exercise apart from the actual playing of the game itself, many do. For instance, Biriba da Costa, the South American champion, plays other sports, including soccer. So do the Swedes. This points up the importance of keeping the legs in good condition. It is far more important to have strong legs than strong arms in table tennis. *The legs must be trained* (*See* Appendix). But it is no use whatsoever to begin a condition-training program involving running and gymnastics for strengthening the leg muscles just before an important tournament; no increased strength will result, and your playing standard may actually diminish. A certain measure of general condition training and gymnastics, specifically including running, skipping, and similar leg work, *must be a part of the tournament player's weekly program the year round*. A suggested program of circuit training is included as Appendix III, but this should be done in addition to, not instead of, running.

One important aspect of good physical condition is alertness. Primarily, this means not being tired, either before the tournament or during it. It usually helps to get more sleep than usual before a tournament, over a period of two or three days, preferably during the same hours that you will sleep once the tournament begins. This extra sleep will allow for nervousness, and it will build up a reserve to compensate for the tournament excitement. It must be taken during the same hours as in the tournament, since any change in routine can be a shock to the nervous system, and nervousness can affect your game.

This brings up the problem of traveling. Is it better to get that extra night's sleep at home in your own bed and get up early to travel, or get to the tournament site a day early and try to get adequate sleep in a strange environment? Only you can answer this question. Remember, though, that when the tournament is really important, some of the better players arrive several days or even a month before. This allows them not only to get used to their new sleeping quarters, but also to the tournament conditions.

Peace of mind is very important during a tournament. Many players, including the better ones, become upset if the seedings and draw are not to their liking. But the draw is made up to the best of the ability of the tournament committee, who will not change their decision; thus there is no point in being concerned about it. If you do complain, you will merely cause animosity. Let the other players argue with the referee and upset their equanimity; *you* should accept the situation and make the best of it. Don't argue with the umpire, either; he will also refuse to change his decision. You may, of course, request that the umpire be changed—but his decision will stand. While you are holding yourself in check, you might also eschew arguments or controversial discussions with friends and relations both before and during the tournament. Such matters are too taxing for the nervous system.

WARM-UP PRACTICE

With most players, even some of the better ones, warming up, at best, is a very haphazard process. It usually comprises some aimless hitting, and perhaps a game or two. With any luck, all this may well limber up your wrist and arm, but it probably will do little more. It will not include all your repertoire of strokes, and it will not warm up the muscles that you will need to rely on in emergencies. Well-organized warming up includes two parts: general physical limbering up, and stroke play.

There can be little doubt that the body will respond best when it has had a thorough workout. An example of a warm-up program used by the Swedes is included in the Appendix. You may well find this quite ambitious—and if your general conditioning has not yet progressed very far, you may be incapable of it. In this case, you will have to work into it gradually. Start with the jogging— which alone will do a reasonably good job of preparing you for the match—and progress from there.

Once you are warmed up, you must then work into all your strokes. To do this, you need an opponent who is similarly inclined. Go through the entire repertoire. Drive on the forehand and the backhand, against both chops and drives. Chop both sides. Try a few drop shots while driving. Lob while defending, and kill the lobs while attacking. Practice a few serves; many players neglect this phase of warming up completely, and consequently miss a few important points on service. Don't forget, too, to place the ball to both sides of the table when driving.

GENERAL

In addition to strengthening the legs, it is important in table tennis to have flexible wrists. Players should avoid carrying heavy objects before important matches: skiing, carrying suit-cases, setting up tables, motor cycling, and similar activities should all be avoided. After going out-doors, it is important to give yourself plenty of time to get your hands warm again before playing.

The training schedule should be maintained evenly the year round, rather than training more intensively just before a match. This can result in overtraining: your best shot may go off, and your weakest may appear unusually good. Always train for the long haul.

Try to play with a variety of practice partners. Against a partner who is stronger than yourself, you will develop a stability in your play, and will learn what you can fall back on when necessary. Against a weaker player, on the other hand, it is easier to practice the strokes that you find to be weaker, and to experiment with new strokes. If you always play with opposition of your standard or stronger, you may tend to develop a one-sided game. On the other hand, if you always play with weaker players, you may lose consistency and become too bold. Change your partners often.

During and just before a tournament, you should avoid eye strain. Forget about movies and television during this period, and, except for scouting prospective foes, watch as few other matches as possible. Even practice sessions can prove tiring, both for the eyes and body; practice only enough during a tournament to keep limber. If you need a change of spectacles, be sure to have the new ones fitted long before the major tournament, so that you are quite used to them. And do your sightseeing after the event.

The importance of a good diet cannot be overstressed. The usual foods found at tournament sites, such as hot dogs, are relatively difficult to digest; in order to avoid indigestion, they should be bypassed in favor of more easily digested foods. Actually, little should be eaten during a tournament, especially in the hour or two immediately preceding it; see a more detailed consideration of diet in the Appendix. What foods are eaten should be eaten slowly, and thoroughly masticated.

Smoking is a controversial issue. American table tennis players generally attach little significance to it. It should be pointed out, however, that in almost all other branches of sport and athletics, smoking is frowned upon, as it is in table tennis circles in many countries. Quite apart from its long-term effects on the lungs and other parts of the body, smoking reduces one's stamina. If you are an inveterate smoker, however, it will pay you to remember that smoking is prohibited in many sports halls and gymnasiums where table tennis tournaments are held. Enforced abstinence during a tournament can aggravate considerably the state of tension or nervousness that one normally must endure at these functions. If you cannot give up the habit completely, then practice laying off for a few hours per day, so that you can accommodate yourself to the tournament schedule.

6/U.S. Tour by Chinese Team

Under the joint sponsorship of the United States Table Tennis Association and the National Committee on U.S.-China Relations, thirty-four representatives of the People's Republic of China—players, officials, interpreters, journalists, and even a team doctor—visited the United States for two weeks in April 1972. The author was fortunate to have traveled with them for eight days.

Without getting involved in the political ramifications, the ultimate purpose of the visit was "Friendship first, competition second." "We will learn from each other," said the Chinese repeatedly. The success of the visit, in these terms, might best be measured in the gradual relaxation of formality by the visit's end. For example, on their arrival a Chinese was asked, "How do you like the mini-skirts?" The reply was, "We respect the customs of all countries." Towards the end of the tour the answer to the same question was, "Very nice."

From the first time I saw the People's Republic of China table tennis team as it disembarked from the Pan American charter plane at Newport News, Virginia, it was apparent that this was a team, truly a team, not just a group of players. Initially this impression was exemplified by the similar personal appearance and dress. The next day I saw the team aspect emphasized as the Chinese in identical dress entered William and Mary Hall in perfect marching unison with arms swinging freely in time with the music. Before and after each match the Chinese players would shake hands with their opponents and the umpire, and between games go immediately to their team captain for instructions. During the matches the Chinese as a group applauded any outstanding play by both their and the U.S. players. Later I was to see this esprit de corps in practice sessions as the Chinese worked with and helped one another. Contrary to the American practices, which were largely unsupervised and consisted primarily of playing games, the Chinese would work out and warm up by doing physical exercises before practicing as much as an hour at a time on one stroke, without playing any games. Yes, this was a team. Our U.S. players were impressed, and they were following many of these examples before the tour was completed. I think that our future teams will be instilled with some of this spirit as were those on the tour. As the U.S. team eaptain, Jack Howard, stated, "Touring with the Chinese was more valuable than attending five World Championships."

The final tour match record was China 34, U.S. 12. Some of us observed that the Chinese did not use their best serves or the third and fifth ball attacks off their serve. We had seen these in their practice sessions. They didn't appear to be hitting quite as hard or as consistently as they did in practice. It seemed as if they didn't move as quickly and were driven from the table more readily by the Americans than when they were playing against a team mate. One game ended with a Chinese girl serving into the end of the table and, on the next point, volleying a ball well off the table—the only time this was done during any of the competition. When various Chinese players were asked if these losses had been intentional, whether they had been "dumped" or "thrown" in the cause of friendship, each answered, "We always try our hardest." However, it was pointed out that a Los Angeles resident won his match at the University of California, Los Angeles, the L.I. champion won his match on Long Island, a Michigan native won his match in Detroit's Cobo Hall, and in the nation's capital both U.S. national champions won.

Since the Chinese are so much better than we are, we would do well to consider how they achieved their skill. The basic factors seem to be the difference in national attitudes toward table tennis, and a marked contrast between the teams' practice methods. In China, table tennis is the top sport, followed by basketball and badminton, and the Chinese make a *study* of it, much as we do of baseball, football, and basketball; we relegate table tennis here to the status of a game or recreational pastime. There are something like two million tournament caliber Chinese players, while the entire USTTA membership is only slightly over two thousand. The best players are known throughout China and their world champions are respected as national heroes. Table tennis facilities are available almost everywhere in China, including all schools, and our players who visited China saw many youngsters adept at playing in the streets on makeshift tables; on the other hand, the average large U.S. city may not have any places to play. Chinese table tennis receives widespread publicity; rarely are the results of our national championships even published.

Through proper table tennis exercises and training the Chinese have developed fitness, quick reflexes, mobility, consistency, hard hitting, and concentration—in matches with the Chinese the crowd noises did not seem to phase the Chinese, though some U.S. players became nervous and disconcerted. The Chinese spend more time conditioning themselves and helping each other, and have better practice methods. Rather than merely playing games as do the American players, the Chinese practice specific strokes, mobility, serves, serve returns, consistency, hard hitting, blocking, etc. Possibly all of this boils down to one thing: the Chinese take the sport more seriously. It is a matter of national pride and personal prestige.

It was most interesting talking to the Chinese and watching their style of play. On close-to-the-table play the Chinese seem either to hit hard and/or place the ball,

Chuang Tse-tung of the People's Republic of China, World singles
champion from 1961 to 1967, illustrates the beginning of his backhand
and forehand drives.

hitting most balls on the rise, particularly on the backhand. The penhold backhand is as I have described in this book, except that the follow through is more forward— like a hard push with excellent placement. When playing close to the table the Chinese use very little backswing on the forehand or backhand but always employ a complete follow through. The average and medium speed topspin strokes are definitely more up and then forward, rather than the forward and then up described in earlier books. Many Chinese seem to hit most of their strokes in a straight line of about 45 degrees, the angle depending on the height and spin of the opponent's shot. Many chops are hit with topspin using an open racket (bottom of racket closer to net than top of racket) and some start with an open racket and close it gradually (top of racket closer to net than bottom of racket) on the follow-through. The one exception is the loop, which uses a closed racket. Topspin counterdrives are always executed with a closed racket. Hard hits are more into the ball with more forward motion; the blade goes forward with slight wrist snap, and the arm follows through across the opposite shoulder or lower. When driven from the table, the Chinese use a much longer backswing and impart heavy topspin and sidespin. They give the definite impression of hitting each ball for a specific purpose, not just to keep it in play as U.S. players are prone to do.

Even a short explanation of the Chinese strokes would be incomplete without a few words about the serve. As in tennis, the toss of the ball is important. U.S. players generally toss the ball higher when executing a chop serve than they do when hitting a topspin serve; it is readily distinguishable. However, the Chinese toss all serves upward just a slight amount. Their favorite is a short serve camouflaged by varying quick arm and wrist movement so that it is almost impossible to tell if the ball has chop or topspin.

Most of the Chinese use the penhold grip. There is

obviously a big difference between the penhold and shakehands grip backhand drives. The forehand attacking strokes are superficially similar with either grip. However, there are five major differences:

(1) The very grips themselves are such that at the start or beginning of the stroke in the ready position the penholder's racket is pointing down, whereas the shakehands player has his racket either horizontal or pointing up. For the penholder this means that his natural tendency is to hit up (topspin), while the shakehands tendency is either chop or all-around play (topspin or chop).

(2) For a normal topspin stroke, the penholder gets more speed because of his lower starting position. The racket blade at follow through is the same for both topspin strokes—either vertical, parallel to the net, for medium speed hits, or beyond the vertical for harder hits or counterdrives. Thus, with more speed the penholder tends to hit the ball higher or off the table. He must therefore correct for this, either by hitting forward more or closing the racket more.

(3) For both the penholder and the shakehands grips the racket starts at the side of the body. The penholder has the advantage that he can more readily start closer to the body and then stroke out to the side before hitting the ball—an action that adds slight sidespin and makes the ball bounce a bit sideways. Most U.S. penholders start and keep the racket too close to the body. At contact, the racket must be well away from the body as in the shakehands forehand topspin stroke.

(4) To execute the penhold forehand topspin properly the body must come into play. Some shakehands players can do a reasonably good forehand topspin with hardly any body motion at all. If a penholder does this, he's entirely too cramped, particularly on the follow through. Body motion was most impressive with the Chinese, and also with Itoh and the other Japanese champions.

(5) One other basic difference is that of the racket

angle at the beginning of the stroke on the forehand side. The shakehands player generally has a vertical or possibly closed racket. The penhold usually starts with an open racket, which is his natural position. For counterdriving and moving against high balls, however, the racket must be closed. This presents a slight problem to the penholder player. By bending forward from the waist, he closes the racket automatically, but he should *not* change his grip to make the correction.

When the teams were in Memphis, the Chinese held a clinic for the Americans. Since I had to leave before that, I'll paraphrase here what was written by the USTTA President, Tim Boggan, in the national publication TABLE TENNIS TOPICS.

The Chinese clean their paddles with water and sometimes soap. They change their rubber every six months for pips out, and every two months for inverted pips. Most Chinese are changing to inverted rackets because more technology is possible.

On the serve, the idea is to carry the ball with your paddle by using quite a fast motion, the paddle under the ball for chop and over the ball for topspin—so quickly that the opponent has difficulty discerning which it is.

A fast hard serve is mainly elbow.

A spin serve is, naturally, wrist. Americans are too stiff-wristed.

Try to serve so a second bounce is possible on your opponent's court. But, remember, if you want to trap your opponent with a short serve, make sure he knows you can serve long.

To return a serve well, you must watch the ball, not the hand. In any number of countries, coaches are very good at teaching hand deception. You must try to figure out how strong your opponent's wrist is. If it's strong, you'll probably need a more forceful return. After the ball leaves the server's paddle, ask yourself, "How does it bounce?" This will indicate what kind of spin is on it. Backspin initially bounces a bit higher. Topspin bounces more forward.

The Chinese have a kind of chop-block shot with which they can vary the spin. The motion always appears the same, but the ball may have topspin or chop or no spin at all. Sometimes they can block a shot almost as hard as a slam.

To return short, spinny serves, try to push the ball low and angle it with sidespin.

Before hitting a drive, try to relax the forearm. The forehand stroke should not be long. The Chinese do not start the stroke until the ball is on their side of the table. The stress is on extremely fast reaction. They don't anticipate until the ball is on their side. It is very likely that your ball will be blocked back and, should it hit the net, they don't want to get caught in mid-air starting a stroke.

There is talk of our bad habit of hitting baby shots. Americans play too safe. They've got to practice hitting the ball as hard as they can for 5 minutes.

If you can't find a good opponent to practice with, spend time on your serves. The serve is a stroke. If you're not practicing it, you're not practicing a stroke.

Strategy is a matter of who attacks first. Once the Europeans get to spinning, the Chinese are in trouble. So they're taught to attack quickly.

Finally, look for your opponent's good points. Maybe you can learn something. Remember, 80% of all the points are finished before the 5th ball.

It is impossible to determine the future or ultimate result of the Chinese visit, but we do know some of the immediate results. The U.S. general public is already starting to look upon table tennis as a sport instead of merely a game or recreational past time. More colleges and schools are taking an interest in table tennis, adding the sport to their curricula. At least two states have held collegiate tournaments and have started forming intercollegiate leagues. At least three states have formed inter-

Li Fu-jung of the People's Republic of China in a match against Erwin Klein at the University of California Los Angeles Pauley Pavilion.

Erwin with Leah (Miss Ping) Neuberger won the World's mixed doubles championship in 1956.. In this match he prevailed 21-13, 21-16 against the World's singles runner-up in 1961, 1963 and 1965. The umpire is Doug Stewart of New Zealand.

scholastic leagues. The President's Council on Physical Fitness and Sports has incorporated table tennis into its program. Three $10,000 money tournaments are being sponsored within the next year. A demand has been established for exhibitions at department stores and shopping malls. Tournament participation by players and spectators has increased 50%. Equipment sales have increased by about 40%. A world-wide Air Force tournament was held this year. A manufacturers' association is being formed for the promotion of table tennis as a year-round sport.

Wherever the Chinese played, a standard program was distributed. This program contained articles on "A Brief History of Table Tennis," "Table Tennis in the United States," and "Table Tennis in China," all by former USTTA President J. Rufford Harrison, and all of which bear repeating here.

A BRIEF HISTORY OF TABLE TENNIS

Table tennis began in England sometime during the 1880's as an amusement. Played with rackets covered by some lightweight material, most notably vellum, and any available ball of whatever composition, it was a simple game for idle hours.

The game's early development was unwittingly influenced by the United States when an Englishman traveling here discovered a toy ball made of celluloid and introduced it to the play. A few years later, in the 1890's, another Englishman purchased one of those pimpled rubber mats used on store counters for the deposit of coins and a few days later won the English championship with a piece of that mat glued to his racket.

Table tennis languished in most countries until the 1920's. It was still little more than a game when the International Table Tennis Federation was founded in 1926. Then someone discovered that, if he stepped back and chopped under the ball, giving it backspin, he had a good chance of returning a hard hit. Play became more interesting, players more fit and agile. The simple game began to take on the attributes of today's complex sport.

Backspin was initially an asset to the fledgling sport. It introduced possibilities of attack and defense, and the struggle to mount the attack first. Yet, in a short time the choppers were so superior to the hitters that play degenerated. Reducing the height of the net helped, but the number of dull, unenterprising games remained high for two decades.

Japan then entered the arena with a new weapon that reinstated attack almost overnight. Their sponge-rubber rackets applied more topspin to the ball, bringing the ball down and permitting the player to hit the ball harder without hitting it out of play. But hitting harder and applying more spin necessitated even greater fitness, and so a generation of players arose who spent as much time in the gymnasium as at the table.

Even this was not enough. The defenders still managed to slow down the super-attackers. Then, at the end of the 1950's, came the latest major development. Imagine that instead of hitting as hard as possible with just enough spin to bring the ball down, the player puts most of his energy into spin, sacrificing some of his speed. The result is the loop drive, which has almost eliminated defensive play. Players forced back now lob instead of chopping, giving themselves extra time to retrieve the next hit and making it difficult for the opponent to loop. Further refinement has led to a stroke that combines the spin of the loop with the speed of a normal drive. The advantage of attack over defense has become overwhelming.

The Japanese brought another development along with the sponge racket—the penhold grip. No world champion had ever won with that grip before 1952. Since then, the handshake grip used by most western players has been rare in World Championship play. So have western players. The sport has been dominated by Japan's sponge-wielding penhold hitters—and by the Chinese.

The Chinese contradict much of what has already been noted about the sport. They are not all hitters. They don't all use sponge rubber. They don't rely exclusively on spin. They don't all use the penhold grip. The Chinese are the artistic scientists of modern table tennis. They have studied it more, and their study has proved worthwhile. They, with the Japanese, Swedes and Hungarians, have shaped table tennis into an athletic sport that demands from its practitioners the utmost in fitness, strength, stamina, speed and accuracy.

The world-wide popularity of table tennis is constantly increasing. The International Table Tennis Federation now has ninety-four national member associations. The World Championships have become so large that it has become necessary to make it biennial instead of annual. Table tennis is the number one sport in China. It ranks third in Japan and is similarly high in many other countries. It is played on every continent.

TABLE TENNIS IN THE UNITED STATES

Table tennis has been played in the United States for most of the present century, but it was not until the 1930's that any significant organization came into being. A national group, the United States Ping Pong Association (USPPA), was then formed.

In China, ping pong is the name of the sport and has no commercial significance, but in the United States, "Ping Pong" is a trade name, and the USPPA was operated exclusively by the owners of that name. To avoid this commercial tie, the United States Table Tennis Association (USTTA) was formed in 1933. It was affiliated with the International Table Tennis Federation (ITTF) in the following year—the first affiliate outside Asia and Europe.

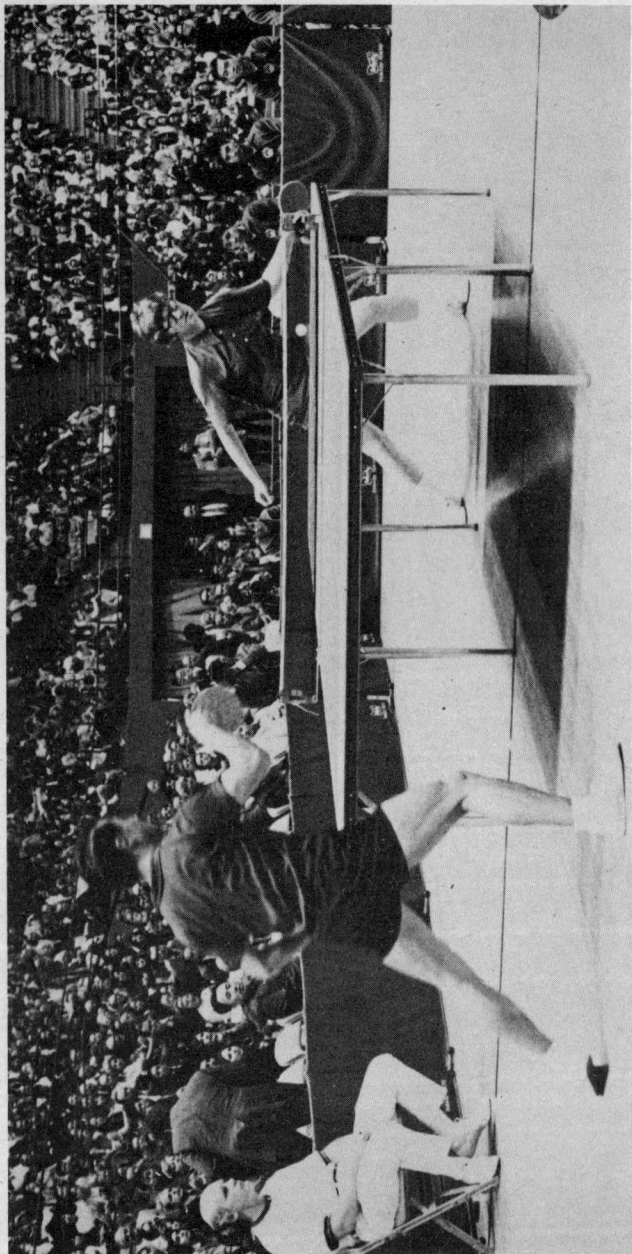

Dal Joon Lee, 5-time U.S. singles champion, hitting a forehand topspin against Ch'en Pao-ching, People's Republic of China, at the University of California Los Angeles Pauley Pavilion.

D-J's heavy topspin was of no avail, losing 21-14, 21-17 to the Chinese close-to-the-table hitter. Both players use the penholder grip and wide stance.

Table tennis was then at a low standard in America, but rapid strides were soon made under the leadership of Sol Schiff, Jimmy McClure, and Ruth Aarons. In 1937, the U.S. became the first country to win both the Swaythling and Corbillon Cups, awarded to the world's best men's and women's team. The Corbillon Cup was won for a second time in 1949.

Ruth Aarons in 1936 won the one United States world singles title. Miss Aarons was in the final the following year with Trudi Pritzzi of Austria, but both players were disqualified for pushing, an unenterprising defensive play. In contrast, the men had developed rapid attacks that led to three doubles titles for the U.S.—by McClure and Bud Blattner in 1936 and 1937, and McClure and Schiff in 1938. Completing the list, the U.S. won two mixed doubles titles: Dick Miles and Thelma Thall in 1948, and Erwin Klein and Leah Neuberger (Miss Thall's sister) in 1956.

In more recent years, the rapid growth of other sports in the country has led to a weakening of the American table tennis standard. The men are currently ranked 28th in the world, the women 21st.

While the U.S. players were influencing international styles of play, they were also helping to shape the rule book. Intense finger spins in service were developed here in the mid-1930's and they immediately began to ruin the sport. The U.S. therefore instituted the flat-hand service rule, and the ITTF quickly followed suit. Towards the end of the same decade, pushing play was making the sport uninteresting to spectators and players alike and the USTTA lowered its nets from 6¾" to the current 6" (15.25 cm.); again, the ITTF concurred. The new rule helped, but some pushing play was still prevalent in the 1960's when the U.S. persuaded the ITTF to adopt its Expedite Rule, designed to accelerate slow matches.

The USTTA is governed by a nine-man Executive Committee, elected by its three thousand members. Local organization is provided by some 130 clubs, organized into district affiliates.

The main functions of the USTTA include the sanctioning of tournaments, selection of teams for international play, ranking of players, coaching, and publication of a national magazine—TABLE TENNIS TOPICS. Its sources of income are principally membership fees and tournament sanction fees; there is no government support.

Information on any aspect of table tennis can be obtained from the Association at P.O. Box 815, Orange, Connecticut 06477.

TABLE TENNIS IN CHINA

The history of table tennis in China begins in the late nineteenth century, but its contemporary significance began in the 1920's. At that time, Mao Tse-tung advanced it as an organized activity in the camps of the People's Liberation Army. Today, it is the most popular sport in all of China.

The Table Tennis Association of the People's Republic of China joined the International Table Tennis Federation in 1953. Its representatives played in the World Championships that year and have since been prominent participants in most international competition with mounting success.

China's first world title came in 1959, when Jung Kuo-tuan won the men's singles. In 1961, he was displaced by Chuang Tse-tung, who repeated his victory in the biennial World Championships of 1963 and 1965. China's men's teams went undefeated in these same years and also won the doubles titles in both 1963 and 1965. They won the Swaythling Cup, presented to the best men's team, in 1961, 1963, and 1965.

China's women were also successful. Chiu Chung-hui won the singles in 1961. The doubles went to Lin Hui-ching and Cheng Min-chih in 1965. In the same year the Corbillon Cup, presented to the best women's team, went to China. Of the seven world titles, China had five.

During the Great Proletarian Cultural Revolution, China's teams did not compete. However, they returned in 1971, slightly weaker but still supreme. That year they again won the Swaythling Cup, the mixed doubles, and the women's singles and doubles—four titles out of seven. They are the world's best.

This high standard is due in part to the number of players in China—easily three million. Their coaching techniques, which have been studied intensively, are also outstanding, and have been their greatest contribution to the sport.

There is a common misconception that all Chinese players are penhold hitters. This is far from correct. They are quite versatile and at the 1971 World Championships, their teams included attackers and defenders, penholders and shake-hand players, as well as wielders of all types of rackets, from inverted sponge to pimpled hard rubber coverings. All were technically, tactically, and strategically outstanding.

CONCLUSION

The author has attempted to cover only the essential aspects of table tennis, the points that he believes are most important in developing the superior tournament player. No instruction booklet alone can do this job, however. It cannot be emphasized too much that the would-be champion will vastly improve his chances of long-term success if he has regular guidance and coaching, preferably by an instructor or coach approved by the United States Table Tennis Association. With this final piece of advice, the author trusts that the reader will benefit substantially from this book. He hopes that the reader will experience improved enjoyment and capability in his practice and play, both before and after becoming a champion. Table tennis is one of the world's finer competitive sports. May you be successful in it!

Appendix

PHYSIOLOGY OF PERFORMANCE: CARDIO-VASCULAR TRAINING

By Frank D. Rohter, PhD

As a gross motor skill, table tennis involves several body parts: the legs provide base stability and transfer of position; the playing arm produces the stroke and the free arm helps sustain body balance; the trunk and neck facilitate upper body rotation; and the forearm and digits grip and manipulate the racket. The co-ordinated movements of these parts are accomplished by the harmonious interplay of the skeletal muscles, the nerves, the sense organs and the higher motor centers of the brain. It is this intimate neuromuscular synchronization that constitutes the skill of playing table tennis.

During table tennis competition, as during any type of exercise, the skeletal muscles in particular experience specific physiological changes. Oxygen is used up and waste products accumulate. One of the functions of man's cardiovascular system (heart and blood vessels) is to transport a fresh supply of oxygen to the skeletal muscles and to carry away the accumulated waste products. During prolonged exercise the use of oxygen and the accumulation of waste products are greatly increased, and the cardiovascular system must respond accordingly. If the cardiovascular system is in a high state of fitness—if the heart muscle is strong and pumps large amounts of blood during each stroke, and there is a maximal number of

98

open capillaries (microscopic blood vessels) bathing the muscle fibers—optimal physiologic limits may be attained. If, however, the cardiovascular system is at a low level of fitness—the heart muscle and the blood vessels are unable to transport an adequate oxygen supply and unable to remove the accumulated waste products that collect at the cellular level—fatigue sets in prematurely and performance is seriously impaired. It seems logical, then, in light of the many hours that championship table tennis aspirants devote to skill development, that they should also be concerned with developing a cardiovascular fitness level conducive to combatting fatigue.

Tournament Play

It is quite apparent that table tennis tournaments demand an enduring day of competition. To begin with, the emotional anxiety caused by the presence of spectators, the challenge of competition, the apprehension of elimination and the pageantry of the playing arena result in a general involuntary tensing of the skeletal musculature during pre-tournament preparation. Therefore, even before the start of actual play the individual performer is somewhat extended, depending upon his level of composure. The cost of pre-tournament energy and the output of work during actual play may escalate total energy expenditures in the skeletal muscles as much as fifty fold.

During the tournament, when play becomes exceedingly strenuous, the body burns up more oxygen than the cardiovascular system can supply. In order to meet these excessive oxygen demands, the body calls upon reserve capacities derived from lactic acid metabolism within the muscle. Two factors are important in this regard: First, although lactic acid metabolism provides a supplementary source of energy, its duration is limited to around twenty seconds, depending on the individual's physiological tolerance to the metabolic by-products; the metabolic by-products of lactic acid produce fatigue at the cellular level. Secondly, the energy derived from the lactic acid metabolism produces an "oxygen debt" which must be repair during the rest periods between scheduled games and matches, otherwise the body will perform submaximally during subsequent bouts of competition. It is at this stage that cardiovascular fitness becomes so important: if both contestants are of equal skill, the better-conditioned player will hold a decided advantage as he will have recovered from previous matches more adequately than his adversary. Moreover, as the tournament continues, the "oxygen debt" builds up and complete recovery becomes exceedingly difficult. Consequently, relative cardiovascular differences become progressively more significant as the contestants reach the finals, and by the championship match the "fit" contender will be able to perform with far greater precision than the "unfit" player.

At this point it seems appropriate to point out that the contestants are continually fighting with the spectators for a share of the limited oxygen supply in available room air in order to guarantee an adequate oxygen intake during play and during recovery. It should therefore behoove all tournament officials to insist on optimal auditorium ventilation and to prohibit spectators from smoking so as to provide maximal oxygen availability for the contestants.

Cardiovascular Training

The first step toward understanding cardiovascular training is to be able to distinguish between strength training, skill training, and cardiovascular training. "Isometrics," "weight lifting," and other terms in these categories are associated with strength-building programs. They serve to increase the tensile strength of muscular fibers and thus enhance the body's muscular power potentiality. Skill training, as discussed previously, involves neuromuscular co-ordination and is developed by executing specific reinforcing performance maneuvers. Cardiovascular training conditions the heart and blood vessels to respond to the increased physiological demands during exercise.

The relative emphasis on strength training as compared to skill training seems to vary according to the particular type of activity in question. To activities like shot-putting, discus throwing, wrestling, and football muscular power may be paramount, while to finer neuromuscular activities such as table tennis, skill may be more significant. On the other hand, all athletic activities need be concerned with cardiovascular training; it is the cardiovascular system that provides the functional nourishment essential to continuing all endurance pursuits, whether they be power activities or delicately skilled activities.

In designing a cardiovascular training program for table tennis athletes there are three general physiological concepts to consider: (1) The heart and blood vessels have remarkable adaptation powers and can adjust, if trained properly, to any realistic physiologic work load imposed upon them. (2) Body structures such as muscle, bones, and blood vessels develop only if stressed. (3) Cardiovascular development is specific—that is, only the body parts conditioned will experience adaptation. In light of premise number three, it becomes clear that in addition to prescribing a training program that develops the heart it is also imperative that the training program should be concerned with an exercise regimen that will develop the vascularity of the legs because the legs assume the greatest work load during match play. According to premise number two, the training program should be such that the heart will be exerted to its physiological limits in order to gain strength, so that the blood will be literally forced through the large muscles of the legs in order to open new capillary beds. And finally, according to the first premise, the body will adapt if stress is adequate.

In my professional opinion, there seems little doubt

that the best way to develop heart and leg circulation is by a prescribed long-distance and sprint-running program. Long distance running, however, poses some significant physiological obstacles. Time schedules, facilities, fatigue, muscular pains, boredom, exhaustion, and weather are all discouraging factors. But if these obstacles can be overcome, *there is no better way to train for the championship table tennis tournament circuit than by a long-distance running regimen.*

The Running Program

There are several things to bear in mind when you launch a running program. First, start gradually and arrange a definite, convenient time schedule. It is easy to become discouraged and to stop training. Therefore, it is advisable to start slowly, maybe ½ mile within 10 minutes for the first day. This may be increased very gradually each day as you grow stronger and can tolerate longer distances. Second, it is imperative that it be a regular routine; irregularity will encourage excuses and the program will soon terminate. Third, arrange to run with a fellow player or if possible a group of players; socializing relieves the monotony of running. Fourth, select a scenic route; this will make the running sessions more enjoyable. Fifth, keep records of your time and distances run so you may use your progress as a motivational factor. Sixth, within your physiological and psychological limitation escalate your running schedule to guarantee the needed cardiovascular stress for development. This may be accomplished by increasing your distance. If, during some phase of the training program, you have pushed too hard and your muscles ache, or you are tired, take a day off, but start again immediately, no matter how bad the weather, or how inconvenient it may be. Remember, regularity is essential to the program. Seventh, as your training program advances you should vary your pace. When you are running at a submaximal pace, you may continue for many miles; however, if you increase your pace to a near all-out effort, you will tire within 10 to 20 seconds. Under these all-out conditions your energy supply is chemically changed and is limited to very short periods of activity. You will soon recover, however, and be able to continue. The sprint or all-out bursts of running should be introduced in the form of a *jog-sprint-jog* routine once you feel you are ready for a more grueling workout.

Both distance training and sprint training are essential to developing high levels of cardiovascular fitness because of the two sources available for energy, viz., that supplied by oxygen in the blood (aerobic) and that supplied by lactic acid metabolism (anaerobic—without the presence of oxygen). The former is enhanced by opening up more capillaries (by distance running); the latter is enhanced by increasing one's tolerance to the lactic acid metabolic by-products (by sprinting).

Summary

The value of cardiovascular fitness to optimal skill performances during a long table tennis tournament has been clearly established. The best training program for developing an efficient cardiovascular system consists of a regimen of long distance and short all-out sprint running. With the development of a high level of cardiovascular endurance, the table tennis athlete will be able to attain maximal efficiency from the table tennis skills that he has mastered. Consequently, he will be more capable of a championship performance throughout tournament play.

DIET FOR THE ATHLETE

By Bill Toomey, U.S. and World Decathlon Champion

One of the most important aspects of training is preparation. A modern-day athlete is quite different from his older counterpart in that he approaches his training scientifically. What was once considered intensive training is no longer even a moderate workout. Present-day performances make it obvious that much has changed. Athletes of today are bigger and stronger and have more stamina. What is responsible for the super athletes of today and for their super performances?

Answers to this question are manifold, but one of the reasons has to be advanced nutrition. The addition of supplements to our diet has indeed been a help to many. It must be admitted that some athletes do not take supplements, but this does not invalidate a need for them by many men and women.

In my experience, the difference between my college-day performances and post-college performances was made possible partly because of better nutrition. As an undergraduate, I was a faddist who believed in being a little underweight for training. I weighed about 168 pounds at that time. Subsequently, with a high-protein diet and more training, I have been able to develop better muscle tone, and now have a body that weighs between 195 and 200 pounds.

What happened to my performance level after the addition of this thirty pounds? Well, in every event in my competitive campaign my performance rose to a much higher level; I developed more speed and a fantastic amount of strength, and was able to maintain a significant level of stamina in longer runs.

The point I am trying to make is that in modern days it is possible to add to one's physical prowess through better nutrition. The reason that many countries of the world fall behind the major powers in the area of sports is that most of their populations exist on a poor diet. Too many individuals have a high carbohydrate diet and insufficient protein for their physical development. These people are characterized by lower stature and poorer bone development.

There should be no question as to the importance of good diet. After all, the human being is the end-product of the fuel that he takes in. Would a person who has invested thousands of dollars in a sports car use a lower grade of gasoline? Of course not. So you, as a human being, must provide your organism with the maximum nourishment possible, especially if you are under the stresses that training exerts.

There has been quite a controversy over the vitamin topic here in the USA. Some people seem to feel that a tremendous amount of money is wasted on vitamins. This author has a different opinion. For the best efficiency in training, one must be subjected to stresses well above the normal. Dosages on vitamin packets are geared for the average person. Any athlete who trains falls into a different category and must therefore establish his own daily requirements. I consider vitamins to be an insurance policy, and therefore provide myself with an over-adequate amount.

At this time I should also like to describe briefly the type of meals that my decathlon roommates and I eat during the day.

Breakfast is usually made in a blending machine. Ordinarily it will include three eggs, three heaping tablespoonsful of protein powder, fruit juice, a tablespoon of calcium lactate, and a small amount of vegetable oil or wheat germ oil.

Our lunches seem to be quite typical: usually a hot main dish, fruit juice, vegetables, jello, and perhaps some pudding. Actually at this stage of development I am not really avoiding too many foods, although I don't have an overabundance of starches such as cakes and potatoes. As a supplement to lunch I add a good portion of desiccated and defatted liver tablets, equivalent to the nutrition found in about two ounces of liver.

Dinner is a big meal and always includes some form

of meat (not overcooked), a vegetable, a salad, and a baked potato. Ice cream seems to be included fairly often also.

Because weights and training schedules vary, it follows that the diet will be varied. Every athlete has his own particular needs. Furthermore, since we all adapt differently to stress training and fatigue, some people have systems that require little food while others continually burn fuel. The best gauge is how you feel in training, and whether or not you seem to be hungry.

An athlete who trains at an intensive level must have the fuel intake to provide his body with building blocks. Burning up calories at fantastic rates and putting the organism under great stress means that in order to build, one must replenish the body with what it needs. The average citizen who works at a desk doesn't have the same problem as the athlete who is constantly working towards physical development. It has finally been recognized today that athletes are different animals and even have special medical needs, as evidenced by the development of sports doctors throughout the world.

My advice to interested athletes is to contact a national coach and ask for details on where he can provide himself with check-ups and physicals to determine how he is reacting to his training. In my event, the decathlon, I train so vigorously that it has been necessary to keep a constant check on my health. The athlete of today is not afraid to train effectively, but in order to achieve the higher plateaus he must also keep a tap on his lifeline and provide himself with the best building blocks available.

Daily Intake of Supplemental Vitamins

Vitamin A	25,000 USP units

B Complex
Vitamin B1	10 mg
Vitamin B2	15 mg
Vitamin B6	10 mg
Niacinamide	100 mg
Pantothenic acid	130 mg
Choline	100 mg
Inositol	100 mg
Folic acid	0.1 mg
Biotin	25 mg
Vitamin B12	25 mcg

Vitamin C   975 mg, increased to 1300 mg for heavier workouts. The same amount of Bioflavaonoids accompany this vitamin.

Vitamin D	2500 USP units
Vitamin E	105 Int. units

Elements
Calcium	800 mg
Iron	10 mg
Copper	0.5 mg
Iodine	0.15 mg
Magnesium	15 mg
Potassium	25 mg
Zinc	0.5 mg

CIRCUIT TRAINING

The program described here was developed by coaches of the Swedish Table Tennis Association. The five exercises suggested are not intended to be restrictive, but are selected merely to ensure that the muscles a table tennis player is called upon to use most frequently are developed to the utmost.

Figure A shows five exercises. In (a) the player should jump as high as possible from a position with one foot back, and should land with the feet reversed. Figure (b) is a standard push-up, and (c) is a standard sit-up, the body being raised until the hands fit easily over the knee-caps. In (d) the player crouches from a standing position, jumps back to the extended push-up position and back again, and returns to his starting position. And (e), which looks the easiest, is simply a stretching of the ankles; it is most important in this last exercise, however, to be sure to rise fully onto the toes.

To carry out the circuit training, first take each of these exercises in turn and determine how many times you can do it in one minute. If you cannot keep going for a full minute, then merely determine how many times you can do the exercise before tiring. Whatever the number, write down one-half of it. Thus, for instance, if you can do exercise (a) fifteen times and exercise (b) eight, then write down seven and four, respectively. Determine these numbers for each exercise separately, with a rest between each pair of exercises. Having done all that, carry out exercise (a) rapidly the number of times that you have written down, proceed immediately to (b), and go through all five exercises in this way, rapidly, three times. Measure the time that you take for this.

Such practice should be done at least twice a week, and preferably daily—it will take less than ten minutes per session. After a few sessions, you will find yourself more efficient, and your time will decrease. When it de-

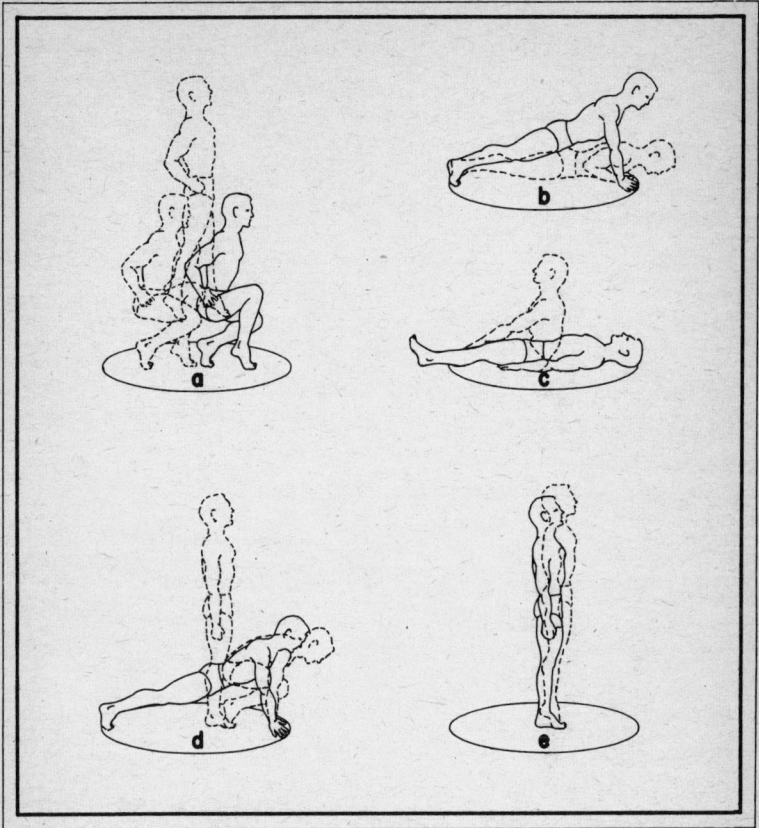

Figure A

creases by 10-20 per cent, then go back to the beginning, and again measure how many times you can do each exercise in one minute. Then proceed as before.

WARM-UP EXERCISES

The body will never produce the best results during the first few minutes of activity. A player should therefore never begin a match without having first warmed up. It might be thought that this work-out could be normal play, on a practice table. However, it is very difficult to be sure that all the muscles that could be called into play during a match are limbered up during ordinary practice. For this reason, the better players go through rather complicated warm-up programs, designed to ensure that they are limber enough for any emergency that can occur during the play.

Figure B diagrams a typical warm-up program recommended by the Swedish Table Tennis Association. Obviously, others could be used just as well. If you have neve done any warm-up work before, and perhaps very little circuit training, you will find these exercises at first rather exhausting. You may therefore wish to begin this sort of thing gradually, doing only the jogging on the first day or two, before adding the other exercises one by one. The entire program should take 15-20 minutes for it to yield the best results.

The following is a brief description of the various exercises:

1. Jogging.
2. Head rolling. Make a complete circle, from side to side and from back to front.
3. Elbow rotation. Bend the arms completely, and rotate the elbows in both directions.
4. Arm rotation. Same as no. 3, with the arms outstretched.
5. Back bending. Keep the knees straight, and touch the floor alternately in front of each foot.
6. Arm bending. Turn the head as you alternately bend one arm and straighten the other.
7. Jumping. Jump as high as possible, pulling up the knees at the same time.
8. Side bending. Bend from side to side, stretching the arms as shown.
9. Knee bending. Pull up one knee as you rise onto the toes of the opposite foot and raise the opposite arm.

Figure B

10. Leg rotation. Lying on the back, raise the feet until they are about six inches from the floor. Then rotate them in both directions.
11. Trunk rotation. Bend the trunk through complete circles in both directions.
12. Jogging again, or this time skipping.

About three minutes spent on each of these will give the optimum performance.

RACKET SURFACES

By Dick Yamaoka

In the early 1950's table tennis achieved reovlutionary changes in techniques by the introduction of sponge. Because of the nature of sponge it became possible to produce more speed and spin. These features of sponge were further stressed by putting the rubber turned outward or inward on the sponge, i.e., by the invention of the regular sandwich and the inverted sandwich. From these changes the basis of the modern table tennis game of speed and spin was developed.

According to the Laws of Table Tennis only three kinds of racket blade rubber surfaces are approved: the pimpled rubber, the regular sandwich, and the inverted sandwich. Nowadays, in this country as well as around the world, a great majority of the players use so-called sandwich, the regular sandwich, and the inverted sandwich. In spite of the importance of the type of racket best suited to particular styles of play, discussions of the characteristics of these rubber types have not been given in table tennis books. This chapter is written with the intention of providing that information, with the hope that it may give the readers a better understanding of the rubber features and help the readers to select the proper type of racket surface best suited to their own games.

Since the main differences between the pimpled rubber
and the sandwich is the sponge, in order to understand
the characteristics of the sponge rubber, the sponge itself
must be discussed. Although both the regular (pimples
out) and inverted (pimples in) sandwich rackets are
called sponge, the sponge used should be clearly dis-
tinguished from the type sponge you will find in your
kitchen or bathroom. The latter has the texture of poros-
ity and air can travel freely from one place to another
place of the sponge. On the other hand, sponge used
in sandwich has the cellular texture, made up of count-
less numbers of tiny cells, with gaseous material inside
and completely surrounded by the thin layer of rubber
and unable to escape from it. When pressure is added,
not only the material of the sponge itself, but also the
gas inside the tiny cells react, and thus the strong elastic
property of sponge is produced. You have probably ex-
perienced this before. Suppose you play table tennis in
winter and the racket itself is rather cold. When you
hit the ball initially, you feel as though the rubber is
"dead." You cannot acquire the fast-ball speed, and you
cannot get the amount of spin you usually do. The
reason for this is that, due to the low temperature, the
volume of the gaseous material in the sponge reduced
and acted with less elasticity than it usually does. This
can be easily corrected either by warming the rubber by
moderate heat or by playing. According to Mr. Tamasu,
the president of a renowned table tennis company and
an outstanding coach, the material used for the sponge
is almost identical to the material used for the rubber.
Because of the gas trapped in the material, it is apparent
that the sponge has more elasticity than the rubber and
thus produces more speed on the ball than the pimpled
rubber. At the same time, since the sponge is much
softer than the rubber, it also allows more contact area
with the ball at the moment of impact, thus giving more
spin to the ball than pimpled rubber alone.

As a general principle, the offensive players prefer to have more speed and spin. This could be achieved by using a very thick sponge. However, the total thickness of the sandwich cannot exceed 4 mm; thus, rather hard sponge is preferred by them. In order to get maximum speed certain manufacturers produce sandwich with thin rubber of about 0.8 mm and hard sponge of about 3.2 mm thickness. On the other hand, for defensive players, the speed may not be of prime importance and sometimes is even undesirable. Instead of speed the defensive players prefer to have better control. Thus, the soft and/or thin sponge is preferred by them.

Pimpled rubber. At the moment of impact the contact with the ball is made at the tips of the pimples. In general, the rubber with small short pimples gives more control while the rubber with large tall pimples gives more speed and spin. Pimpled rubber cannot produce the amount of spin and speed produced by sandwich. However, it gives the best control and shows the least reaction against the opponent's spin. The main feature of pimpled rubber is the steadiness and better control one achieves with it.

The question is often asked, What is the difference between the regular sandwich and the inverted sandwich? Although both use sponge and give more speed and spin than pimpled rubber, they have unique features.

Regular sponge rubber. At the moment of impact the pressure is delivered to the sponge through the rubber which lies on the surface of the sponge, thus displacing the sponge. The rubber on the surface of the sponge has the effect as though the sponge were a little harder. The ball will be expelled with the elasticity of sponge, with some help from the elasticity of rubber, thus giving more speed to the ball. In addition, since the contact with the ball is made at the tips of the pimples, it will give good control, and gives less reaction against spin. In general,

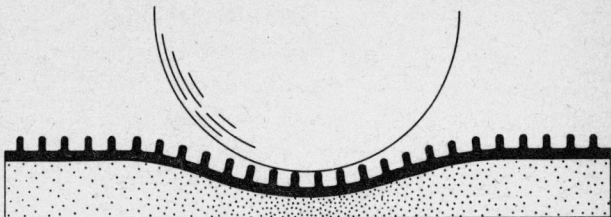

REGULAR SANDWICH

THE SHEET AT THE BASE OF THE RUBBER GIVES THE EFFECT OF HARDENING THE SPONGE, AND THE RUBBER BECOMES STRETCHED. THIS WILL GIVE EXTRA SPEED.

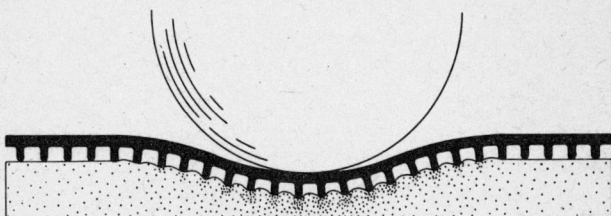

INVERTED SANDWICH

PRESSURE IS TRANSMITTED THROUGH THE TOPS OF THE PIMPLES. NOTICE THE FORM OF THE SPONGE SURFACE.

Figure C

regular sandwich with small pimples gives better control, and the one with large pimples gives more speed.

Inverted sandwich. At the moment of impact the pressure will be delivered to the sponge through the tips of the pimples, thus giving closer enclosure to the ball compared to the regular sandwich. At the same time it gives the largest contact area with the ball, thus producing very strong spin. The amount of spin is closely related to the condition of the surface of the rubber. In order to get maximum friction from the available material, certain manufacturers use pure rubber as material for the rubber. Since the characteristics of both sponge and rubber are fully utilized in this, it may be said that the inverted sandwich is the most advanced rubber available at present. In general, the one with densely distributed short pimpled rubber gives more speed, and the one with coarsely distributed high pimpled rubber gives more spin. While the main feature of the regular sandwich is its speed, the main feature of the inverted sandwich is its spin.

	control	speed	spin
pimpled rubber	A	C	C
regular sandwich	B	A	B
inverted sandwich	C	B	A

In the above table three rubbers are compared in three properties—the control, the speed, and the spin; they are graded by A, B, and C according to the order at each property. Thus, the amount of spin produced is largest with the inverted sandwich, and least with the pimpled rubber. It indicates that the reaction against the spin is largest with the inverted sandwich and least with the pimpled rubber. In relation to the table, it must be pointed out that these properties are labelled by A, B, and C based on the relative comparison, not based on the absolute evaluation. For example, the difference in speed between the regular sandwich and the inverted sandwich will be barely distinguishable. Furthermore, the chart does not say that the speed and spin cannot be obtained by the pimpled rubber at all. As a matter of fact, considerable amount of spin and speed can be given by pimpled rubber.

The above table, together with the effects of thickness and hardness of the sponge as considerations, gives the readers the basis for the selection of the rubbers best suited to their games. For offensive players who use a relatively large swing and use strong spin and hard drives with the help of footwork, the inverted sandwich will be the desired racket. Since this is the style of play employed by large numbers of offensive players in Japan, the inverted sandwich is used by many Japanese offensive players. For offensive players who stay close to the table and develop a high pitch offense, as do most of the Chinese offensive players, the strokes are rather short and the ball must be hit in a shorter period of time. At this position, very little time is allowed to judge the amount of spin on the oncoming ball; therefore, good control becomes a rather important factor. When close-to-the-table hitting is used, it will be understood that the best-suited rubber would be the regular sandwich. In fact, most of the Chinese offensive players use the regular sandwich. I mentioned before that speed is an important factor for offensive players. That is the reason most offensive players use the sandwich rubber. However, for offensive players who always stay very close to the table and use fine net play and quick attack, the weight of control will be more important than the speed. Thus, for certain types of offensive players the pimpled rubber is recommended. For the all-around players whose main style is the controlling game with all types of strokes, rather than spinning or hard hitting, the pimpled rubber will be best suited.

While the basis of the offensive game is speed and spin, the basis of the defensive game is spin and steadiness or control. For the steady type defensive players, the best rubber will be the pimpled rubber, which has the best control and the least reaction against the spin. For the defensive players who use strong spin, the inverted sandwich is recommended. Since the speed is not only unnecessary but also undesirable for most of the defensive players, softer and rather thinner sponge sandwich is recommended. For the players who have distinctly different forehand and backhand styles of play, the rubber selected should be based on the styles of play for each side. For example, a few of the best players in the world today use their backhand as only a defensive weapon for chopping, pushing, or blocking; either pimpled rubber or regular sandwich is better suited for this type backhand. The forehand rubber will vary, depending upon the style of play. If the forehand is primarily defensive with a controlled offense, pimpled rubber may be best suited. If the forehand is used as more of an all-around weapon using chop, hard drives, and counterdrives, regular sandwich is generally preferred. If the forehand is used primarily as an offensive stroke using spin, speed loop drives, lobs, and counterdrives, then inverted sandwich is the desired rubber.

Since the rubber plays such an important part in the performance of your play, you must always pay particular attention to the condition of the rubber, and the rubber should be replaced periodically. When to replace the rubber should be based on the condition of the rubber rather than the period of its use. The wear on rubber is dependent on the style of play, the type of rubber used, the thickness of the rubber, and the period of its use. A former world champion, during the time he held the title, changed the rubber once a week. According to one of the officials at the 1967 World Championships, the members of the champion Japanese team averaged rubber replacements once a month. These may be rather extreme cases. However, if you play table tennis several hours a week, in general it is a good idea for you to change the rubber at least every six months.

For the pimpled rubber, the best way to judge the condition of the rubber is at the base of the pimples. When the pimples show cuts at their bases, it is time for rubber replacement. When you hit the ball with the part of the rubber in this condition, you will be able to feel the different reaction and generally lower than your normal standard of play.

For the sandwich, you must give your first attention to the condition of the sponge. After repeated contact with the ball, some of the gas contained in the sponge may escape and lose some of the elastic power of the sponge; this starts to show the sign of the "dead" reaction, i.e., the feeling of less spin and speed. When you hold the racket and bounce the ball all over the surface and you can feel the difference in bounce from the middle part of the racket (where the contact with the ball is made most frequently) to the other parts, then it is time to replace the rubber. In addition, for the regular sandwich, the same conditions must be made that are applicable to the pimpled rubber. For the inverted sandwich, the condition of the surface of the rubber must be carefully inspected. When the surface of the rubber shows a difference in friction from the center to the other portions, the rubber must be replaced. The condition of the surface is especially important for the inverted sponge because this determines the amount of spin given to the ball.

Due to the popularity of the inverted sandwich, the proper maintenance has become one of the main concerns of many players. It is speculated by many that the regular sandwich lasts longer than the inverted sandwich. However, when proper care is taken for the surface of the rubber, the inverted sandwich will last longer than the regular sandwich. The racket should always be kept in the case when it is not in use. It will be ideal if the case is moisture

proof. Not only is this good for the rubber, but it is also
good for the racket blade and may eliminate the possible
formation of a crack in the blade. Under any circum-
stances do not expose the rubber under the direct sun for
a long period of time, and do not expose the racket to
extreme heat, because either of these two conditions may
melt the material of both the rubber and the sponge. You
will often find that the surface is covered by dust, which
is of some concern because it will reduce the frictional
effect of rubber. When you clean the surface of the rubber,
always use soft tissue with plenty of water. Avoid press-
ing hard to the rubber while rubbing off the dust and other
foreign particles. Rub slowly and use just enough pressure
to remove the dust, so that the rubber friction will not be
affected. After the cleaning has been completed, shake
the racket to shed it of excess water and then let it dry.
During tournament competition it is often observed that
the players wipe the surface of the racket with the hand
by moistening it with perspiration or saliva. This must be
avoided for the proper care of the rubber. It is known that
perspiration will react with rubber and erode it. Saliva is
not good for the rubber either. By touching the racket with
your fingers grease may be deposited on the surface, and
once grease has been deposited it is very difficult to remove. Even a slight trace of grease on the rubber will
give a different reaction from the normal friction. When
the surface of the rubber accumulates deposits and they
cannot be removed by water, apply alcohol to remove
them in the same manner as you would with water. Use
soft tissue with plenty of liquid, and give just enough
rubbing pressure to remove the deposits. Once the racket
is cleaned, avoid touching the surface with your fingers as
much as possible. Since there is the possibility that the
rubber may be affected by chemicals, the use of these
liquids should be kept to the minimum frequency. It is
recommended that the perspiration be wiped from the

rubber at the end of the day in order to prevent the rubber from becoming eroded.

SUGGESTED OUTLINE FOR A COACHING COURSE

The following describes a recommended sequence of player development, which has been used with excellent results. It is not intended to be exclusive; neither is it essential to include everything written here, or to carry out each stage in the order listed. Pupils and coaches vary widely in their preferences. It is, however, strongly recommended that a coach not permit his pupil to advance to a later stage until he has fully grasped all previous stages.

The coach should endeavor to develop a close rapport with each pupil right from the start. Praise here, correct there, but always encourage. The amount of correction given to any pupil in any lesson should be restricted. Most pupils cannot manage to pay attention to more than three items in any one session.

Footwork

Explain first the reasons for correct footwork: (a) Correct footwork is an essential constituent of all proper stroking. It permits correct form to be achieved earlier; (b) Correct footwork is the easiest part of the game to learn early, and *the most difficult to correct later*.

Of course, the footwork for each shot will be discussed as it is first introduced, but the generalities mentioned in Chapter 1 should be covered here. Explain the relation between footwork and the correct shift of the pupil's weight during the stroke. In fact the whole subject of stance, body movement, and follow-through should be covered at this time.

Wall practice is a good way to introduce footwork. Mark a line on the floor perpendicular to the wall. If the ball bounces on one side, the pupil should attempt to perform a backhand stroke, and a forehand stroke if it bounces on the other side. Be sure that the follow-through on all these strokes—whether good or bad—is long. This wall practice will present a good opportunity for the player to gauge the effects of spin, which should be explained early in the course. Be sure that he knows what effects spin has, while the ball is in motion in the air and when it hits a table or racket surface.

This first lesson covers all the fundamentals. Limiting it to wall practice and footwork has the advantage that there is nothing here that the pupil cannot do at home on his own. And he will do that if he is at all eager. He can also obtain valuable information about his strokes by practicing before a mirror; photographs will also help.

Services

Explain the potency of the service. It is so powerful a stroke that the service and its return should be covered in a lesson restricted to these topics.

Begin with footwork, on forehand and backhand topspin and chop services; sidespin can be added later. Review spin theory, and stress observance of opponent's racket during service. Later, explain how to disguise the spin. Throughout all this, perform the services first yourself, explaining the spin that you are imparting. Then have the student copy.

The Push

So far, the student has not played any table tennis and he may well have dropped out of the course. If so, he is not the type who could have persevered, and you need not regret his loss. Begin with correct footwork and the chop service, and demonstrate the push, using both forehand and backhand. Use only moderate spin until the student is consistent. This practice will develop consistency, and also—if the coach perseveres—good footwork. As the student progresses and can handle more intense spin, add sidespin.

Backhand and Forehand Kills

Introduce the kill early, to give the student a feeling of accomplishment. Demonstrate the footwork, racket angle and follow-through. Start with the backhand, since most players are weak on that side. Cover change of pace and placing, which can be as useful as outright speed. And be sure that the kill, more so than all other shots, is consistent.

The Block

With little backswing and follow-through, the block is not glamorous, and teaching it may not be easy. Persevere with it. It is an excellent shot for use in an emergency or for controlling the game. Remember the block on the forehand side.

Drives

Starting with the backhand, review footwork, and practice the drive swing before a mirror. The stroke is essentially a lenthened block, starting earlier and finishing later. Start by feeding the student relatively easy, high chops, and be sure that his follow-through is smooth. Review the body roll and the shift of weight. Be sure the ball is contacted at the height of bounce or earlier.

Chops

As with the drive, start with the backhand or the chop in front of the body, these being typically weak. Emphasize consistency before spin, but eventually teach a slight addition of sidespin. Be sure that the student does not attempt to make contact too early, and stress the sideways stance.

Counterdrives

Once again review spin and the importance of topspin. Have the student drive from close to the table while you block from a convenient distance. Then gradually convert your blocks to drives, and finally move to the table, gradually forcing the student farther back, *still driving*. In this way, be sure that he can counterdrive from any distance. Be sure that he uses enough topspin to provide enough margin for error, with enough follow-through for control. On the backhand, check that the student moves to the ball, without undue reaching. Check that the stance is more square than when driving a chop.

General Techniques

Throughout all of this training, and through that which follows, it is, as we have mentioned before, important to maintain a good rapport with the students. Provide encouragement where due and praise where appropriate, interspersing these with constructive criticism. This latter should be directed to no more than three points per session if it is to be effective.

In the practice of all strokes, be sure that the student does not get into the habit of playing from only one position; for instance, many players limit their forehand drive practice exclusively to crosscourt shots from the right half-court. Be sure that the stroke can be directed both cross-court and down the line, from either side and from the middle, and not neglecting the shot directed directly at the opponent.

In developing this practice, the student will have to learn how to change the angle of his shot. This point alone will be worth a separate session.

Twenty-five-Time Check-Out

After the basic development of any stroke, a criterion of achievement is necessary in order that hitherto undisclosed errors can be uncovered.

Have the student attempt to keep the ball in play for 25 consecutive hits, while you return it easily, using only half of the table. Try this on all shots, and in all directions. Do not permit the student to progress far beyond any particular stroke until he can pass this test.

Five-Time Check-Out

This is like the 25-time check-out, except that the coach should attempt to make the student miss. Play within reason, however; use only those shots, and those variants of them, that the student is supposed to be already familiar with. A common error that this check-out, and the previous one, will reveal, is a tendency to hit or chop too hard. Do not omit these tests; they will teach patience.

Drop Shot

Start by having the student push balls that happen to be low and short, and then explain, and have him practice deception, holding back the drop until the very last instant. Be sure that the grip is relaxed on this shot. Warn about routine drop shots that are easy to anticipate. Be sure that the student practices hard, well-placed drives on the stroke after the drop shot, but have him also learn to perform consecutive drops. Explain the use of the shot against the long defender or the tired defender.

Also practice drop shots against topspin. Check that the second bounce of the drop shot is over the table.

Advanced Drives

Vary your chops from heavy to light and from low to high, and ensure that the student can vary his drive accordingly. He should use his hard drive only when appropriate, should not drop shot too frequently—in particular, he should not use the drop shot as a means of overcoming poor footwork—should not offer a set-up when presented with stiff chop (check that the racket is not open), and should vary his pace and direction.

Advanced Chops

Now reverse the roles, vary your drives, and have the

student chop. Have him stay as close to the table as possible to minimize the effects of the drop shot. Explain that it is easier to chop hard if the ball has intense topspin, but encourage him to vary the chop on all types of ball. Check that his returns are low and deep, and varied in direction. Encourage an occasional counterdrive with as much topspin as is convenient.

The Lob

Especially if your student is essentially an attacking player, encourage him to develop a lob defense. Points of note here are direction—mainly to the backhand—height, and spin. The racket will have a tendency to be open, but this should be resisted as much as possible. Do not permit the pupil to use sidespin on this stroke until he has mastered its use exclusively with topspin.

Attack Against the Lob

Using only topspin initially, lob to the student and encourage him to hit at the height of the bounce. He should strive for placement rather than force to start with, but should later hit harder and shorter, in order to give wider angles and greater height to the rebound. When he is consistent at hitting to both wings, add sidespin on the lob. Have him also practice blocking the ball, i.e., drop shotting.

Loop drive

This stroke is quite difficult to teach and to learn. If the student has developed a good lob with topspin, the loop should follow naturally by stroking nearer to the table and more forward. If not, have him practice by dropping the ball from shoulder height to the floor, and skimming it over the net on the rebound. Watch for the open racket, and listen for it too; the loop is almost inaudible when performed correctly with a closed racket;

look also for a swing that is too early or too short. Start with the slow loop, which is performed with an almost vertical swing, but graduate from that to faster versions of the stroke, made by swinging more forward with a more closed racket. Permit no wrist in this stroke until its other motions have been learned consistently.

Encourage placement, which is difficult until the unusual arm-action has been fully learned.

Special Practice

Half-table Practice. Play a few games or a complete practice tournament using only half of the table. The half can, of course, be a diagonal half or a half down one sideline. Be sure that the players use correct strokes during this play, rather than forgetting them during the excitement of competition.

Counterdrive Practice. Apart from the return of service, require the players to return every ball with topspin. Check that the stance is relatively square. A natural tendency is to hit every ball hard—often too hard. Stress safety and speed variation. Be sure that the student moves to the ball, especially on the backhand where many tend to reach too much. Encourage the student to move back when facing a hard hit, and forward when the opponent is forced to hit slowly. When the opponent hits very hard, the student should incorporate the lob into this practice.

Mobility Practice. With one player chopping or top-spinning everything, the other should use only his backhand or only his forehand. This restricted player may be further required to perform particular types of stroke, such as all topspin. A good deal of footwork is needed in this form of practice, which is therefore excellent for doubles. It will also give the student a wider variety of strokes, and will prevent his being caught completely out of position during a game.

Other practice with Special Rules. All manner of special rules may be devised to encourage players to develop their weaknesses or to make them think. For instance, alternate pushes with drives; hit two balls to the right and one to the left; drop shot the third ball; and so on. Care must be taken to ensure that routines of this type do not become so entrenched that they are played the same way in a match. Practice in this way can be part of normal coaching, or, if both players are given a routine, it can be made part of a match.

Ready to Conquer

It is very difficult for any player to reach beyond a certain plateau unless he has a better player with whom to practice. Players should therefore always be encouraged to play with weaker players part of the time. Such play can be used to develop the strong player's own weak points, or else, with handicaps, it can be used as an inducement to the weaker player.

Nevertheless, it is possible to become better than the available players. The world champion managed it. It can be done by the method mentioned in the previous paragraph. If several players are all of about the same standard, some will nevertheless be better than others in one or more shots, and deficient in some other aspects of the game. These weaknesses can always be developed by playing with peers or with weaker players, so that the player's overall standard will gradually rise.

In addition to all this practice, there is much to be gained from watching other players, especially champions, and from talking with them and discussing their games with others. Such observation, combined with practice and with self-analysis, needs only natural ability and the will to win, and the student will be *ready to conquer*.